Public Speaking
In A Week

Matt Avery trained as an actor, and speech and drama practitioner, and has trained people in public speaking for all occasions, all over the world. Matt also lectures in motivational speaking.

To my mother.

My sincere thanks to everyone who contributed to this book with details of their experiences, and to those whose support made it possible, especially Suze and my family.

Public Speaking In A Week

Matt Avery

First published in Great Britain in 2013 by Hodder Education. An Hachette UK company.

This revised, updated edition published in 2016 by John Murray Learning

Copyright © Matt Avery 2013, 2016

The right of Matt Avery to be identified as the Author of the Work has been asserted by him in accordance with the Copyright, Designs and Patents Act 1988.

Database right Hodder & Stoughton (makers)

The *Teach Yourself* name is a registered trademark of Hachette UK.

British Library Cataloguing in Publication Data: a catalogue record for this title is available from the British Library.

Library of Congress Catalog Card Number: on file.

Paperback ISBN 978 1 473 61030 9

Ebook ISBN 978 1 444 18627 7

1

The publisher has used its best endeavours to ensure that any website addresses referred to in this book are correct and active at the time of going to press. However, the publisher and the author have no responsibility for the websites and can make no guarantee that a site will remain live or that the content will remain relevant, decent or appropriate.

The publisher has made every effort to mark as such all words which it believes to be trademarks. The publisher should also like to make it clear that the presence of a word in the book, whether marked or unmarked, in no way affects its legal status as a trademark.

Every reasonable effort has been made by the publisher to trace the copyright holders of material in this book. Any errors or omissions should be notified in writing to the publisher, who will endeavour to rectify the situation for any reprints and future editions.

Typeset by Cenveo® Publisher Services.

Printed and bound in Great Britain by CPI Group (UK) Ltd., Croydon, CR0 4YY.

John Murray Learning policy is to use papers that are natural, renewable and recyclable products and made from wood grown in sustainable forests. The logging and manufacturing processes are expected to conform to the environmental regulations of the country of origin.

John Murray Learning
Carmelite House
50 Victoria Embankment
London EC4Y 0DZ
www.hodder.co.uk

Contents

Introduction

**Public speaking is the ritual humiliation of one person by a
group of onlookers before whom he or she must orate, laying
themselves open to embarrassment, belittlement and ridicule.**

Does this sound about right?

If it does, then it's time to do something about it because
public speaking really doesn't need to be an ordeal. It can,
and should, be stimulating, self-affirming, empowering and
even enjoyable. It can also provide a great boost to your self-
confidence and to your self-esteem, the benefit of which can
be enjoyed in all aspects of your work life, and beyond. Not
only that, but accomplished public speakers are much valued
and sought-after by the majority of businesses, who recognize
that excellent communication skills are a key tool in today's
workplace.

Mastering the art of public speaking, then, will strengthen your contribution to your company, and your perceived value within it, as well as boosting your confidence and providing you with a new and exciting outlet for your skills. So what type of public speaking are you hoping to excel at?

Whether you need to present to just a few people at an in-house meeting, or to thousands at a global conference, the principles are the same, and once you have mastered them you will be able to use them in a variety of situations. You will find that your self-belief receives a healthy boost when you can stand in front of an audience and confidently deliver a speech with clarity, dynamism and panache. You will also find that over time your voice becomes stronger and clearer, allowing you to make yourself noticed and heard in *any* situation. In turn, your contribution to your company will be better heard and acknowledged, fully realized and even rewarded.

As you develop a reputation within your company as someone with excellent public speaking and presentation skills, you may even find yourself being asked to present on the company's behalf at conferences and seminars. This can be a great way to get yourself noticed, both in your company and beyond, and can provide a very useful entrée to networking. It's also a consummately transferable skill which can help to make you an attractive acquisition should you at any time decide to move on from your current employment.

So there are a great many reasons to want to become excellent at speaking in public – but is it possible to learn how to do it? And is it possible to do it in just one week? Happily the answer is 'yes' because public speaking is an art, not a science. It doesn't matter what your current level of experience or ability might be – with diligent practice of the techniques in this book you will be able to master the art of engaging, dynamic public speaking in just seven days – and then reap the rewards for years to come.

SUNDAY

Writing
your speech

Good public speaking does not require stimulating material – it requires that the material you have is delivered in a stimulating way. And this means that it needs to written and structured in a stimulating way. Depending on your subject matter, it may not be possible to fill your speech with exciting material – but it's always possible to ensure that you compose your speech in such a way as to make it interesting to listen to. To do this, you will need to adhere to some fundamental principles, and it's worth investing the necessary time early on to ensure that the material you are going to deliver – the speech you hope people will want to listen to – is as good as it can be.

Preparing a good speech, and in good time, will also help you to combat any nerves you may experience (and it's highly likely you will, since these, left unmanaged, are one of the most common roadblocks to good public speaking).

Finally, it's important to remember that material that is written to be spoken is very different from material that is written to be read, both in style and content, and mastering the techniques for writing a great speech will in turn help you to master the techniques for great delivery.

The basics

What makes a great speech?

There is a difference between making a great speech and making a speech great. Making a great speech requires fantastic delivery, whereas making a speech great requires fantastic writing. Of course, it naturally follows that the better your speech is written the more likely it is that you will be able to deliver it to maximum impact. So let's look at how to write a great speech.

There are three stages to writing a successful speech:

1 Tell them what you are going to tell them.
2 Tell them.
3 Tell them what you have told them.

If this sounds like a recipe for a repetitive and boring speech, remember that your audience won't be familiar with the material, as you are, and in some cases may not even be familiar with the subject area, so it's important to give them every opportunity not only to listen to what you are saying but to take it in. Following this simple three-stage approach will also ensure that you adhere to two basic principles of speech-writing:

1 All the information you want to convey should be **confined to the body of your speech.**
2 Audiences need to hear your key message **at least three times** for it to really sink in.

Of course, you will need to tailor your format to your audience (e.g. if you will be addressing a mixed group, some of whom are very familiar with your subject and some not at all, you will need to find suitable middle ground so as not to bore the former or leave the latter stranded) but you should always aim to structure your speech in three distinct sections:

1 introduction
2 speech
3 conclusion.

Introduction

This should comprise no more than:

● introducing yourself to your audience
● introducing your audience to the key tenets of your speech.

It's important that you keep the introduction to just that, an introduction, and that you don't begin to explore any of the topics your speech will cover. By introducing all the key areas of your speech you are ensuring that nothing in your speech will come as a surprise (unless this is intended – and this is a technique that should be used rarely and sparingly), which in turn means that your audience will be prepared and should therefore be receptive to what you have to say.

Speech

This is the main body of your material and should contain all the key parts of your speech – everything you want people to take away from your speech should be here. You will introduce the themes, and go over them again in your conclusion, but this is where they should be described in detail.

Conclusion

This is your opportunity to sum up the key points and reiterate them so that they stay firmly in your audience's mind. Don't try to go over everything you've said – keep it tight and focused on only the main points – and don't ever try to introduce new points here.

Getting started early

Proper planning and preparation prevents poor performance.

The earlier you start working on your speech, presentation, or whatever form of public address you will be giving, the better your delivery will be. It's a common mistake to believe that preparing your material in good time is important only to ensure that what you are saying is as good as it can be.

In reality, preparing your material in good time also allows you to ensure that how you say it is as good as it can be. Leaving it to the last minute, or, worse still, just 'winging it' on the day, is a recipe for disaster.

When it comes to public speaking, there is no such thing as being over-prepared.

Preparing your speech in good time allows you to become familiar with your material. This is crucial for good, confident public speaking as it:

- allows you to lift your head from your notes and speak directly to your audience, making all-important eye contact
- gives you confidence in your delivery, knowing that what you are saying is interesting
- allows you to read from brief, headline notes and memory joggers, so that you don't have to write out the entire speech and read it verbatim
- ensures that you can stay calm, relaxed and in control without the fear of losing your place and stalling your delivery
- helps to settle your nerves since you can go into it well-practised and sure of your ability to do a good job
- ensures that you don't omit anything important, which you then have at the back of your mind for the rest of your speech
- ensures that you don't ad lib, which serves only to give an impression of unprofessionalism – unless you are very, very good at it
- gives you the time and opportunity to rehearse your speech so that you're familiar with every aspect of it.

Prepare well, and prepare early.

Initial preparations

Since it's never too early to start, there are a number of things that you should get under way right now. These will help you to focus on the task ahead and prepare some necessary groundwork:

1 Begin sketching out a **draft plan** of your speech – however rough. This should be regularly updated.
2 Ask any colleagues, bosses, stakeholders and so on. whether they want to be **consulted** on your speech. If there are specific items they want you to include, then the sooner you know about it the better.
3 **Know your audience.** This is important so that you can pitch your speech appropriately – so if you're not sure who will be attending then find out.
4 **Begin practising speaking out loud** – and loudly – whenever you're on your own. At first, it will sound odd to you but the more you do it the more normal it will become.
5 Line up some **willing volunteers** in front of whom you can practise making your speech, preferably people who are used to public speaking and from whom you can receive constructive criticism.

While a friend or partner may seem an obvious candidate, a colleague with a knowledge of your subject area is likely to be a better choice since they are better placed to spot any errors, superfluous material or repetitions – and they are likely to be less forgiving and more vocal in their criticism!

Starting and finishing strongly

You don't need to be a professional speech-writer to write a great speech. By thinking about what you want to say well in advance, structuring your thoughts carefully, and continually improving your speech over time, you will soon discover that everyone can write a great speech.

Get into the habit of always carrying with you a pocket-sized notebook devoted exclusively to your speech and jotting down thoughts as and when they occur to you. You can structure them later – the important thing is to capture them before you forget them.

The beginning and end of your speech are the parts that are likely to be most clearly remembered so you will need to make sure these are particularly strong.

It's crucial to have a **strong start** to your speech in order to:

● grab your audience's attention
● help them to relax (which will help *you* to relax)
● break the ice
● make your audience want to listen to your speech.

It's crucial to **finish strongly** in order to:

● bring your speech to a definite conclusion
● ensure a smooth handover to the next speaker (where applicable)
● end on a high note
● leave the audience wanting more.

Structuring your speech

You will need to divide your speech into sections so that it takes your audience on a journey. What this looks like will, of course, depend on the material you are delivering but try to ensure that your speech flows neatly from one section to the next. By breaking it down in this manner you will make it easier for:

● your audience to follow
● your audience to digest
● you to focus on the key content in each section.

You will also need to give some thought to the length of your speech. Making the speech unnecessarily long is a trap into which inexperienced speech-givers commonly fall, in the mistaken belief that:

● they will appear in command of their subject by demonstrating the scope of their knowledge
● they will have time to 'get into it' and calm their nerves
● they will give their audience value for money
● there won't be time for any awkward questions and answers!

The truth, of course, is that the value of the speech lies in the quality, not the quantity, of the material and, crucially, in the quality of the delivery.

> *A short, punchy speech delivered with dynamism, with a few key messages that shine out, will be remembered long after an endlessly wordy, albeit worthy, speech has been forgotten.*

Keep your speech short, relevant and 'fat-free' and your audience will thank you for it. It will also help to ensure that your message is clearly defined, and that it does not get lost in a jungle of superfluous material padding out your speech.

'If you can't write your message in a sentence, you can't say it in an hour.'
Dianna Booher, US communication expert

Remember that:

- a short speech...
  - will be more memorable
  - will leave the audience wanting more
  - might be a pleasant surprise!
- a long speech...
  - may make the audience restless
  - can appear self-indulgent
  - is likely to obscure the important points.

> *Don't forget that your speech may not exist in isolation – and that any audience has a maximum tolerance for listening! Your audience may already have heard one or more speeches and may have more to listen to after yours, so make your speech stand out by keeping it tight, focused and punchy.*

Setting the tone

'They may forget what you said, but they will never forget how you made them feel.'

Carl W. Buechner, US theologian

When writing your speech it's important to bear in mind how you want to come across to your audience – not simply how it sounds to you. Think about whether you want your speech to be regarded as:

● authoritative
● sincere
● professional
● humorous
● no-nonsense
● friendly
● insightful
● witty

... and so on. In reality, you will probably want it to be a mixture of several things, and it easily can be, but you must be careful to avoid a mixture of tones cancelling each other out so that your speech just appears bland. In order to avoid this, you will need to ensure that you:

● decide what the predominant tone of each section should be
● keep each section defined and unique
● begin and end on an upbeat note to hook your audience.

It's certainly important to inject some colour into your speech since orations without variety, interest and impact are difficult to listen to and easy to forget. Striking the right balance between writing a speech which is dry and dispassionate and one which is gushing and effusive is a fine art, but one which will make all the difference between an end product which is run-of-the-mill or truly memorable.

Writing your speech – advanced techniques

To give your speech that extra dimension that will elevate it above and beyond the majority of speeches, and make it truly memorable, you will need to employ some more advanced speech-writing techniques. Remember that many members of your audience may well listen to speakers on a regular basis, so to stand out from the crowd you will need to use some 'tricks of the trade' which will help you to change a good speech into a great speech through a process of enhancements and fine-tuning.

Fine-tuning

Great speeches aren't written, they're rewritten. You simply can't expect, or even hope, that you will be able to compose a great speech at the first attempt. Even if you plan the outline with great care and precision and then work diligently over time to fill in the blanks, you can be sure that the speech you end up with will be markedly different from your first draft (it may even bear no resemblance to it at all!). This is because you will need to employ a continual and ongoing process of revision and reworking, fine-tuning your speech by crafting it until you have smoothed off all the rough edges.

'Great speeches aren't written, they're rewritten.'

The most effective way to do this is to revise your speech regularly, and often, keeping it always somewhere at the back of your mind and practising delivering it at every opportunity, even when this is just inside your head (e.g. when out for a walk or at the gym). This will help you in a number of ways.

For example, you will:

● become **increasingly familiar** with your material, ultimately allowing you to give your speech with minimal need for notes and enabling you to maintain eye contact as much as possible

- become increasingly used to delivering your speech, helping to **settle your nerves**
- be constantly on the lookout for ways in which your speech **can be improved,** particularly by adding important material you had overlooked and deleting any extraneous material.

It's impossible to overstate the importance of removing any, and all, material which doesn't need to be there. Material which is simply acting as padding, which is unnecessary filler, which serves no particular purpose, may be repeating a point already made or which you will make better elsewhere, which creates 'run-on' sentences by not knowing when to stop so that the sentence would clearly have been punchier and easier to listen to and better remembered if it hadn't been allowed to go on so long, material which repeats itself, material which goes on too long, material which repeats itself, which starts to appear in love with the sound of its own voice, which repeats itself and goes on far too long...

You get the picture? This is one of the most common pitfalls in speech-writing, often because people worry that they won't have enough to say, or because they are (often subconsciously) creating a quantity of material which they hope will compensate for a lack of quality, either in the speech or, more usually, in their ability to deliver it. Sometimes people simply want to include every relevant fact and overlook the crucial point that they don't need to say everything they know on any given topic in every speech.

Indeed, falling into any of these traps of including too much material is hugely detrimental since your audience will simply start to tune you out! You have probably experienced this yourself when listening to an uninteresting speaker drone on and on and on, or someone who simply tries to convey far too much information in their speech. No matter how hard you try to concentrate on what they are saying you find your mind wandering, and their material, no matter how good, is wasted. Worse still, if some of the speech is good but surrounded by an obscuring mask of detritus they run the risk of all of it being lost.

SUNDAY

MONDAY

TUESDAY

WEDNESDAY

THURSDAY

FRIDAY

SATURDAY

The best way to counter any of these potential pitfalls is simply to keep going over your speech and honing it: reworking, editing, paring, rewriting and recrafting until it's lean, interesting and the right length – not for you, but for your audience. By doing this, any pointless material or repetition will stand out a mile and you will find yourself wanting to cut it before it begins to grate, or to bore you. In this way you will be keeping only the very best all the time, and by adding to it as and when thoughts occur you can also be sure to cover all bases, while being ever mindful of keeping it to an appropriate length.

'Always be shorter than anybody dared to hope.'

Rufus Daniel Isaacs, 1st Marquess of Reading,
barrister and British Foreign Secretary

When new material occurs to you, capture it immediately. You can work out later on where best in your speech to put it – the important thing is to make sure that you get it committed to paper before you forget it.

Sometimes you will want to leave your speech for a few days to gain perspective, and this can be very valuable (provided it doesn't become an excuse for not working on it!), but it's important not to leave it too long, or too frequently. Try to get into the habit of updating your speech on a regular basis; otherwise, you might go for weeks without looking at it if you don't think of anything new to add to it. In particular, try to ensure that you revisit your speech after:

● presenting it to anyone who is helping you to practise
● adding new material (check for repetition)
● leaving it for a few days (to gain perspective).

At the very least, you should aim to revise your speech once per week. If your command of the subject is excellent (which should be taken as read if you are going to speak publicly on it), and if you are continually thinking about how to improve it, then you shouldn't find the process of writing your speech too difficult or daunting.

> ### 'Grasp the subject, the words will follow.'
> Cato the Elder, ancient Roman statesman

Injecting variety

Any audience has a maximum tolerance for listening, so it's a good idea to add some variety to your speech to help break it up, particularly if it's lengthy or one of several speeches to which your audience will be listening that day.

Good ways to achieve this include:

● using props
● showing slides
● playing music
● showing video clips.

SUNDAY

MONDAY

TUESDAY

WEDNESDAY

THURSDAY

FRIDAY

SATURDAY

Be careful not to overdo it! If your entire speech is filled with props, slides, music and so on, then this becomes the norm and ceases to add variety.

Adding variety helps to keep your speech fresh and differentiate it from any other speeches. It also:

- creates interest for the audience
- breaks up your speech
- divides your speech into sections.

Remember to use only things which are directly relevant to your speech, and support or embellish it.

By thinking this through at an early stage you can ensure that everything you use is really justified and not just there for show, and that it's properly worked into your speech.

Where possible, it is also a good idea to add some **humour** to your speech. This can be a great way to:

- break the ice
- add variety
- help your audience to relax
- help you to relax
- keep your audience entertained – and thus engaged.

Tailoring your speech to your audience and venue

If possible, you should try to get some idea of the people who will comprise your audience so that you can tailor your speech to suit them. Pitching a speech at the right level is crucial for ensuring that your audience:

- don't get bored by hearing things they already know or that they don't understand
- hear something genuinely new and interesting
- remember what you have said.

In the same way, if you have the opportunity to scope out the venue beforehand, it will help you to tailor your speech to the specifics of the venue:

● **For a very large venue with a sizeable audience:**
You will need to remember that not everyone will be able to see your face so don't rely on this to communicate feelings or ideas – make sure they are obvious from your words.

● **For a very small venue with a small audience:**
This can easily become overly familiar, or preachy and worthy – you will need to ensure that you write your speech with a suitable degree of formality and so on.

Summary

However good you are at public speaking, your overall performance can only ever be as good as the speech you have written allows you to be. Of course, a bad speech can be delivered with panache and dynamism, but it will still be a bad speech. Imagine how much better it would have been if the speech itself had been good to begin with. So the quality of the speech you prepare will be a limiting factor in determining how good your performance will be, and how memorable your speech will be.

In addition, knowing that you have a great speech to deliver will help to build your confidence for the moment when you step up to deliver it. Having a really interesting speech removes a good deal of the pressure on you as a speaker since you will not need to 'sell' your speech to the audience, but rather to ensure that they have every opportunity of hearing it clearly and delivered with confidence.

The speech you write will therefore form the bedrock of everything else to do with giving your speech, so it really is worth investing the necessary time and effort to get it as good as possible.

Tomorrow we will begin to master the art of delivery...

SUNDAY
MONDAY
TUESDAY
WEDNESDAY
THURSDAY
FRIDAY
SATURDAY

Fact-check [answers at the back]

1. Your speech should...
a) Dot your themes about in a random fashion ❏
b) Employ a clear, linear structure ❏
c) Simultaneously cover as many topics as possible ❏
d) Make it difficult for your audience to follow so they will have to concentrate ❏

2. The key themes of your speech should...
a) Be confined to the introduction ❏
b) Be confined to the main body of the speech ❏
c) Be confined to the conclusion ❏
d) Be in the introduction, the main body of the speech and the conclusion ❏

3. With public speaking it is...
a) Poor practice to prepare too much in advance ❏
b) Good to practise a little ❏
c) Good to practise a lot ❏
d) Impossible to be over-prepared ❏

4. To begin with, speaking aloud when you are on your own will seem...
a) Entirely natural ❏
b) Odd and ridiculous ❏
c) Better than remaining silent ❏
d) Comforting ❏

5. It's crucial to have a strong start to your speech in order to...
a) Grab your audience's attention ❏
b) Remind yourself what your speech is about ❏
c) Make sure that the microphone is working ❏
d) Wake everyone up ❏

6. Your speech should take your audience on a journey because...
a) Everyone likes a story ❏
b) It makes it easier for your audience to follow ❏
c) They may be unfamiliar with the local area ❏
d) They probably don't get out much ❏

7. It's preferable to keep your speech short because...
a) There is less chance of making mistakes ❏
b) If your delivery is boring, at least there will be less of it ❏
c) It will be more memorable ❏
d) You get paid the same anyway ❏

8. You will need to go back over your speech because...
a) You may have omitted something vital ❏
b) You may have included something untoward ❏
c) Great speeches aren't written, they're rewritten ❏
d) You never get things right first time ❏

9. It's good to inject variety into your speech because...
a) Otherwise your speech will be boring ❑
b) Your audience may have poor concentration ❑
c) Everyone loves juggling ❑
d) It creates interest for the audience ❑

10. It's good to tailor your speech to your audience so that...
a) They are not being told things they already know ❑
b) It can't be used again ❑
c) It can't be plagiarized ❑
d) They can keep up if they are slow ❑

MONDAY

The basics of public speaking

For many people, simply standing in a large room and speaking out loud seems very odd and even rather disconcerting. Hearing your own voice – loud and the only sound in the space – can be very off-putting at first, and it's something you will need to get used to, and comfortable with, before speaking in public.

It's essential that you are at ease with this element of public speaking as it forms the bedrock for the more advanced techniques we will look at later on – without it, it will be extremely difficult to employ successfully the methods which will captivate and inspire your audience. Happily, it's something you can get used to fairly quickly and easily, as are learning to command the space and eliminating bad habits.

Other techniques such as using the actor's method of projection and supporting your voice take a little longer to master, but they are perfectly achievable – and if you are willing to put in the hours you will be amazed just how much progress you can make in one week.

As you master the techniques set out in today's chapter, you will begin to develop your own style and, importantly, grow in confidence until the thought of feeling embarrassed at hearing your voice bouncing off the walls is just a distant memory.

Getting used to speaking aloud

There is only one way to get used to speaking out loud and to hearing the sound of your own voice (which will at first sound and feel unfamiliar to you) and that's to do it. Try it the next time you are alone – **if you are alone now then read the rest of this chapter out loud.** At first you are likely to feel:

● self-conscious
● that you're showing off
● acutely aware of the sound of your voice.

This is natural and to be expected and will wear off only with repeated practice, so every time you find yourself alone try speaking out loud.

Most people are rarely conscious of hearing their own voice in everyday situations, but when it's the only sound in the room and everyone is listening to you you will hear it in a whole new light – and it's something you need to get used to.

It doesn't matter what you say – the object of the exercise isn't to practise your speech but just to get used to the actions of speaking aloud. So don't be put off by not being able to think of anything to say; say whatever comes into your head or, alternatively, just grab a book or newspaper and start reading it aloud.

Don't worry if you feel ridiculous (and you almost certainly will at first), just keep going – it's only with repeated exposure that you will begin to feel comfortable with hearing yourself speaking out loud, and if you can't get comfortable with it in this environment just imagine how you are going to feel when you have an audience looking back at you – and listening to your voice.

Try speaking out loud whenever you are on your own. This will:

● force you to concentrate on your voice
● give you an opportunity to get used to hearing yourself
● make it seem normal!

Rehearsing in front of other people

SUNDAY

MONDAY

TUESDAY

WEDNESDAY

THURSDAY

FRIDAY

SATURDAY

'All the real work is done in the rehearsal period.'

Donald Pleasence, English actor

Practising giving your speech in front of a small, invited audience is vital preparation for giving your speech in front of a real audience. You can start with just one person and build up to a few colleagues, family members or close friends. Initially, you are likely to feel:

- nervous
- awkward
- embarrassed
- self-conscious.

This is entirely natural (indeed, it would be unnatural if you didn't!) but it will subside with practice and experience, leaving you free to concentrate on delivering your speech with dynamism and élan; and this will give you the best possible chance of ensuring that your message is heard and remembered. You might even be pleasantly surprised and find that you *enjoy* giving your speech. And remember that it's far better to get past this hurdle now than to face it for the first time when you are standing in front of an expectant audience.

Using cue cards

One of the most important techniques to master for good, confident public speaking is the use of cue cards. By having the outline of your speech written out in front of you, you will have the reassurance of not having to remember your entire speech – something which is a recipe for disaster no matter how good your memory is, since the pressure of the occasion can make the minds of even the most confident speakers go blank. Equally disruptive to fluent public speaking is to have your entire speech written out in full for you to read to your audience. Doing so provides a number of unnecessary potential pitfalls:

● It will be difficult to establish and maintain good eye contact with your audience since your eyes will necessarily be cast down most of the time, reading.
● Spontaneity will be lost if you are reading verbatim and your audience might just as well sit in their seats reading a copy of your speech instead of listening to you delivering it.
● Your speech-giving can all too easily morph into a homily, making it seem condescending or overly worthy to your audience.
● It's easy to lose your place in a speech which you are reading word for word, and this can cause an embarrassing hiatus, making both you and your audience nervous.

While you should, broadly speaking, stick to the script and avoid improvisation, it's always a good idea to tailor your speech to each audience, perhaps including something topical or particularly relevant to the place in which you are speaking. This is much easier to do if you are speaking freely from headline overviews than if you are reading aloud an essay.

So what makes a good cue card?

Depending on the length of your speech, it's likely that you will need a number of cue cards, and this can be used to your advantage to help you break your speech down into manageable sections. Always keep in mind that a good speech is one which is easy to listen to and remember, as well as one which is easy to give. By breaking your speech down into logical component parts you will be making it not only easier to deliver but, crucially, easier for your audience to receive.

So your speech is likely to consist of a stack of cue cards, each focused on a different area of your speech, and each containing sufficient information for you to know instantly what you will be saying next without providing so much that it causes you to pause while you read what you have written.

The secret to creating a great cue card can be broken down into seven points:

1 Size
It should be sufficiently large to fit enough information that you avoid the need to move on to a new card every two minutes, and to enable you to use a size of writing that you are able to read easily at a glance. It should also be small enough that it fits comfortably in your hand and doesn't obscure your audience's view of you (that is particularly important if you are speaking from a raised dais).

2 Clarity
The clearer the words on the page, the clearer your speech will be. It's a simple fact that, if you can glance at your cue cards and glean all the relevant information in a moment without breaking stride, then your speech will remain fluent and easy to listen to. To achieve maximum clarity you will need to:

- use a clear, easy-to-read typeface
- keep the text large enough to read at a glance
- underline all headings and subheadings
- highlight key words and phrases in the text
- use plenty of spaces and line separation to prevent the text from becoming too dense
- clearly number each card in sequence
- mark each card with a coloured dot in one corner using a different colour for each section (important if you are giving a long speech covering a number of different subject areas).

3 Detail

How much information should each bullet point contain? Include too much and you will find it hard to see the wood for the trees – and there is a very real possibility that you will simply end up reading aloud what you have written, verbatim. Include too little and you may well find yourself struggling to remember what exactly the point was that you wished to make! Therefore, including just the right amount of detail is extremely important – how much this is will depend on your preference, your style of delivery, and your ability to recall information (particularly facts, statistics, etc.). To find out what is going to work best for you, simply do a trial run.

4 Focus

By having the topic or subtopic highlighted at the top of each of your cue cards, you will give yourself a handy reminder of the focus for each section of your speech, ensuring that they are always easy to see and always front of mind.

5 Direction

Just as actors have a director to help them to get the most out of their performance, and annotate their scripts in order to remind themselves where they need to go, when they need to pause, and so on, you, too, should mark up your cue cards with similar reminders. Which points require more emphasis? When should you pause? When is it crucial to look up and make eye contact?

6 Quality

This refers to the quality of the card you use and not the quality of your speech, though one should reflect the other. By using really good-quality card you will be able to:

- hold them steady without fear of them bending away from you
- rest them on a lectern without fear of them blowing away
- see clearly what you have written without a strong backlight at subsequent pages showing through
- avoid distracting your audience by them trying to read your notes.

It also helps to convey an image of professionalism which will put your audience at ease. Remember to use smart blank cards with plain backs.

7 Back-up

Plenty of great speeches have been ruined by the speaker mislaying their cue cards. Always ensure that you carry a spare set and always keep the two sets separate. It's a good idea to also carry a memory stick with your speech backed up on it, and, if possible, to have it on a computer back at the office which you can access remotely.

Warning!

Prepare your cue cards carefully, and double-check that everything on them is as it should be. Even one slight error in preparing your cue cards can make all the difference when it comes to *pubic speaking* (sic) and under the pressure of the occasion this can be all that is needed to throw you off balance causing you to stumble over your words, laugh or dry up altogether.

Making eye contact

Establishing and maintaining eye contact with your audience members is one of the most important aspects of good public speaking – of any kind. Any speech-giver who fails to make eye contact with their audience risks distancing them, and leaving them unengaged. Imagine watching someone giving a speech in which they fail to make eye contact and imagine how that makes you feel – and what impression it gives you of them. They will seem disinterested and aloof and you will be far less likely to care about what they are saying.

Making eye contact allows you to:

● engage with your audience
● establish a rapport with your audience
● make each audience member feel included
● deliver your speech with dynamism.

It will also help you to:

- look confident
- look interested
- feel less nervous
- keep your head up!

Failing to establish eye contact creates a damaging separation between the speech-giver and their audience, while making and maintaining good eye contact does the opposite, drawing them in and engaging them. Remember that you don't need to do this all the time, but that the more you can manage it the better your speech will come across.

Addressing a large audience

If you are addressing a large gathering then you might not be able to look directly at each and every member of your audience but that doesn't matter – what matters is that every member of your audience will feel involved just by knowing that you're making eye contact with someone in the audience. Try to move your gaze around so that you take in different people and different sections of your audience as your speech progresses.

Facial expression

Appropriate use of facial expression can be used to help you to convey any number of meanings which will help to support what you are saying. Of course, you will want to avoid your speech turning into a comedy routine of strained expressions and gurning, so the trick is to keep them to a minimum and keep them appropriate. On the other hand, a speaker who is resolutely unanimated runs the risk of appearing disinterested, or even bored, with their own speech!

It's important to do what feels natural to you, so don't force it – just be mindful that, if your face reflects the tone of what you are saying, it will help to support your message, and the audience will be more likely to receive it well.

Correct posture and relaxation

By standing tall, and looking relaxed and confident, you are more than halfway to getting a good reception from your audience. Whether or not this translates into a good response to your speech will depend on its contents and your skill as a speaker, but by establishing the basics early on you will be giving yourself the best possible chance.

If a speaker looks cowed and worried, their audience is likely to be sceptical about their ability to deliver an engaging speech, and also about the quality of their material. If a speaker stands tall and appears relaxed and in control, then the opposite is true.

Avoiding fidgeting

Fidgeting needs to be avoided at all times as it's distracting to the audience and a clear sign of a nervous speaker, as well as taking attention away from what you are saying. The best way to avoid fidgeting is to practise speaking aloud while looking at yourself in a mirror, or better still employ the services of someone to watch you as you practise, in order to identify the ways in which you fidget.

Every speaker is different and will fidget in different ways, so it's important to learn what yours are and then to establish ways of eradicating them. Some of the more common ones are listed in the table below, together with ways to avoid them.

It's important to remember that fidgeting is not restricted to physical movements – it can also manifest itself in other ways, such as nervous laughter, frequent swallowing, unnecessary coughing, lengthy unintended pauses or gabbling, and so on. Try to give yourself plenty of time to identify the problem areas for you and don't be tempted to ignore them, in the hope that they will just go away over time. However tiresome it may be to work on them, it's much easier to do so when you are practising than when you're standing in front of a room full of people, and it really will make a huge difference to the quality of your presentation. Remember the Russian army motto:

'Train hard, fight easy.'
Aleksandr Suvorov, Russian general

Ways of fidgeting	How to avoid them
Shuffling feet, or regularly shifting weight from one foot to the other	Plant your feet firmly, shoulder-width apart, and imagine that they are nailed to the floor. Concentrate on standing tall, imagining a thread joined to the top of your head pulling you up. This will keep your feet firmly planted and improve your posture.
Playing with hair, fiddling with jewellery, etc.	Keep your hands firmly on the lectern or on your cue cards. Playing with your hair or other types of fiddling are often subconscious, so don't allow your hands to wander.
Scratching, or wringing hands	Usually a reaction to nervousness. Ensure that you have employed the relaxation techniques in this book (see Thursday) and remember to take deep, calming breaths, before your speech and during it. Keep your hands firmly on your cue cards or lectern.
Flailing arms	Usually the result of trying to emphasize a point, particularly when you feel nervous about your ability to convey your message. Occasional use of gestures can be beneficial but lots of imprecise movements will only distract your audience so keep your arms still unless you wish to make a deliberate movement – and then make it clear, clean and quick.
Rapid blinking	Employ the relaxation techniques, focus on your key messages, and concentrate on making eye contact with members of the audience. Focus on one person and try to imagine that they are the only person in the audience, and deliver a part of your speech to them. Then choose someone else and do the same... and so on.

Clarity

You will want to make sure that every word you say is heard and understood, and it's important to remember that clarity of speech and careful annunciation are just as important as volume. Trying to listen to someone who mumbles, and trying to understand them and concentrate on what they say, is very difficult and quickly becomes wearing. If your audience have to work hard to understand you, they will:

- be devoting their attention to trying to catch what you are saying rather than to understanding its meaning
- quickly tire and their attention will start to wander
- think less of you as a speaker.

So practise speaking aloud to see if you are naturally clear in your speech.

If you are not, this is something you will need to work on by practising tongue twisters, speaking aloud sections of text ensuring that you clearly annunciate every vowel sound and every consonant, and by strengthening the muscles in your tongue and jaw. You will also need to practise speaking loudly, and make sure that your voice doesn't lose any clarity as the volume increases.

Putting your audience at ease

If your audience is relaxed and comfortable, they will be more receptive to your speech, and the more confident you appear to be, the better this will be achieved. Remember that it doesn't matter how you *feel* – it's how you *look* that counts. A swan might be paddling furiously under the water but on the surface it appears to be gliding effortlessly. By learning to walk confidently to the podium or lectern and smiling at your audience with certainty and confidence, radiating an unshakeable belief in your ability to give a good speech, your audience will relax and you will have achieved a significant victory before you even begin.

Avoid the classic trap for the unwary and inexperienced of telling your audience that you are not used to making speeches, or that you are nervous. Novices do so in the hope that it will:

- lower the audience's expectations
- make you feel better
- break the ice
- get the audience on your side (through sympathy).

It's a mistake which actually has the opposite effect, but it's amazing how often it's made (even by people who are not new to speech-giving!). What saying so actually does is:

- make your audience feel uncomfortable
- make your audience nervous *for* you and *about* you
- undermine your speech
- undermine you as a speaker.

Furthermore, pre-empting your audience's view that your speech won't be good is a great way to ensure that's how they remember it – even if it was actually excellent.

> **'Why doesn't the fellow who says "I'm no speechmaker" let it go at that instead of giving a demonstration?'**
>
> Kin Hubbard, US cartoonist and humorist

Setting the tone

The tone of your speech is crucial to helping you to convey its message in the quickest and clearest way possible. If you include too many 'ice-breaker' jokes or stories, particularly early on in your speech, you run the risk of undermining the content; and if you are hoping to inspire your audience to do something you hope they will see as enjoyable, then an overly serious tone might seem depressing and undermine your message. So it's important to determine:

- the overall tone you wish your speech to convey
- the tone of any individual sections, or subsections
- how you hope your audience will feel on hearing your speech
- what actions, if any, you hope your speech will produce.

Later in the book we will look at some of the ways in which the tone of your speech can be established, but it's important to remember to identify early on what you want it to be.

Keeping to the script

Many an otherwise excellent speech has been undermined, sometimes disastrously, by the speech-giver straying from their script and inadvertently saying something detrimental or damaging. A quick aside, an ad lib, a moment of lost concentration and discipline, and the whole speech can all too quickly go horribly wrong. Often, such asides are the result of nervousness, leading to the speaker trying to add something extra to make the speech more interesting if they feel their audience isn't responding in the way they had hoped.

It's therefore very important to stick to the script. If you are satisfied that the speech you are giving has been as well written and rehearsed as it could be, then you will have every reason to feel confident about it – and no reason to stray from what you have planned to say.

Keeping to your script will ensure that:

✓ you say everything you wanted to

✓ you keep your speech tight and focused

✓ you look and sound confident and in control

✗ you don't say anything you may later regret

✗ you don't dilute your speech with poor material

✗ you don't go on too long.

'No one ever complains about a speech being too short!'

Ira Hayes

Resisting the temptation to hurry

There are four primary reasons why speech-givers feel an (often overwhelming) urge to hurry:

1 nervousness at having to give their speech
2 lack of confidence in their abilities

3 lack of confidence in their material through:
  – fear that it's not sufficiently interesting
  – concern that their audience may disagree or identify factual errors
4 fear about overrunning their allotted time.

It's important to remember, however, that hurrying your speech is detrimental for a number of reasons:

● It can make you appear nervous.
● It makes it more difficult for the audience to hear what you are saying.
● It makes it more difficult for the audience to follow what you are saying.
● It may come across as breathless and disjointed.
● It denies you the important ability to:
  – clearly separate sections of your speech
  – use pauses to add emphasis to important moments.

Therefore, in order to eliminate the temptation to hurry you will need to eradicate the reasons behind it, allowing yourself the freedom to give your speech to the best of your ability, and giving your audience the freedom to listen to it to the best of theirs.

It is good practice to get into the habit of letting out several deep, slow, controlled sighs to completely fill your lungs with air before you start speaking. This will help you to:

● *start with a good strong voice*
● *maintain a consistent flow of air*
● *slow down your heart rate*
● *distract you from being nervous.*

The following table will help you address the usual reasons that lie behind hurrying:

Reasons for hurrying	How to avoid them
Nervousness	Practise the techniques in Friday's chapter, 'Dealing with nerves', and remember that you are likely to want to hurry – so force yourself to go slower than you want to (50 per cent is usually about right).
Lack of confidence in your abilities	By practising the techniques in this book you will soon be able to write, and deliver, a great speech – so focus on that and be confident in your abilities.
Lack of confidence in your material	If you have researched your subject thoroughly and taken the necessary time to carefully write and structure it, you have every reason to be confident that it's both interesting to your audience and factually correct.
Fear of overrunning	Provided you have practised your speech out loud and timed it to ensure that it's a suitable length, you can be confident that you will not overrun. Find out well in advance how long you are expected to speak for, and whether you will be required (or want) to take questions from the floor, and then aim to make your speech 10 per cent shorter.

Practice makes perfect

'It takes one hour of preparation for each minute of presentation time.'

Wayne Burgraff, US philosopher

Delivering a speech well is a skill which needs to be learned and practised. You can master the principles of public speaking in a week but the more you practise – and keep practising – the better you will become. How much practice you will need to put in will depend on a number of factors, including your:

● previous experience
● natural aptitude
● starting level of confidence.

SUNDAY
MONDAY
TUESDAY
WEDNESDAY
THURSDAY
FRIDAY
SATURDAY

The best thing to do is to get into the habit of practising speaking out loud. Try to practise saying your speech out loud, and implementing the techniques you will learn in this book, as often as possible. It doesn't matter where you are or how long you have got – every extra bit of practice will be valuable to you and for several reasons:

- The more often you hear yourself speaking out loud – and loudly – the more natural it will seem.
- The more frequently you practise your speech the more familiar – and more comfortable – with it you will become.
- Practising saying your speech regularly will better enable you to see if and where there are any gaps.

Summary

The basics of public speaking can be quickly learned, and as you practise putting them into action you will begin to develop your own style of delivery. Before long you will be thoroughly familiar with hearing your own voice loud and clear in a room, and confident of speaking with authority to a small audience. Using your cue cards to prompt you, you will be able to deliver your material without rushing, and with a flair which hooks the audience and keeps them engaged.

Remember that many of the techniques in this chapter can be practised wherever you are, and with however much time you have to spare. Imagine that you are on a business trip and find yourself in a hotel room with ten spare minutes – grab the opportunity and start speaking aloud.

Remember that it's not important what you say – you can just read the room service menu – but that you are using the opportunity to practise, practise, practise. Before long you will find that the techniques become second nature, and your speech-giving will flourish as a result.

Tomorrow, Tuesday, we will build on what we have begun today!

SUNDAY

MONDAY

TUESDAY

WEDNESDAY

THURSDAY

FRIDAY

SATURDAY

Fact-check [answers at the back]

1. When you first start rehearsing in front of other people you are likely to feel...
   a) Elated and uplifted ❏
   b) Confident and self-assured ❏
   c) Nervous and self-conscious ❏
   d) Short and fat ❏

2. It's important not to read your speech, but to use cue cards to prompt you, because...
   a) They allow you to maintain good eye contact with your audience ❏
   b) Speaking while reading causes headaches ❏
   c) Cue cards are lighter to hold ❏
   d) You may not be able to read your writing ❏

3. All headings and subheadings should be underlined because...
   a) They act as quick reminders of the key themes in each section of your speech ❏
   b) It makes them seem more important ❏
   c) Your audience may ask to examine your notes afterwards ❏
   d) You need to remember to shout them ❏

4. Establishing and maintaining eye contact with your audience is important because...
   a) If you can see them, they can see you ❏
   b) It allows you to engage with them and make each person feel included ❏
   c) You can gauge their reaction and speed up or slow down ❏
   d) They won't leave if they know they are being watched ❏

5. It's important to look relaxed and confident because...
   a) It will divert attention from your speech ❏
   b) If you rush through your speech, no one will notice ❏
   c) It will inspire confidence about you in your audience ❏
   d) It makes you look sexy ❏

6. Fidgeting is to be avoided because...
   a) It's distracting, and a clear sign of a nervous speaker ❏
   b) It saps your energy ❏
   c) You may lose your place in your speech ❏
   d) It can make your audience dizzy ❏

7. Clarity of speech is important because...
   a) It shows you have had a good education ❏
   b) Your audience can concentrate on *what* you're saying, not just on trying to hear you ❏
   c) It allows you to whisper ❏
   d) You won't need to use a microphone ❏

8. Avoid telling your audience that you are unused to public speaking because...
a) They are likely to leave, to go and hear someone who isn't ❏
b) It will be obvious anyway from your delivery ❏
c) It will make your audience nervous *for* you and *about* you ❏
d) They will still boo if you are rubbish ❏

9. It's important to keep to the 'script' because...
a) It avoids any copyright issues ❏
b) It was written by a professional scriptwriter ❏
c) Your audience has a copy and will be following it ❏
d) It will keep your speech tight and focused ❏

10. Hurrying your speech is detrimental because...
a) You are being paid by the minute ❏
b) It can make you appear nervous, and your message may be lost ❏
c) Speaking slowly allows you to speak more quietly and save your voice ❏
d) You are not supposed to finish before lunch is ready ❏

TUESDAY

Advanced public speaking techniques

Having learned the basic techniques of public speaking, you can now move on to the more advanced practices. These are the techniques which will elevate your speech from solid and professional, to dynamic and engaging. Having your speech heard and understood is one thing, but delivering it in a way which will captivate and inspire your audience is another – and it's this which will mark you out as a great public speaker.

By learning to use expression and inflection to convey meaning and tone effectively, and through mastering the arts of pausing and phrasing to give your speech real clarity and precision, you can deliver a speech which will be easy to listen to and difficult to forget. Add to this the techniques of varying your pace, pitch and volume, learning how to use audio-visual and multi-media materials and props, etc. to best advantage, and how to spotlight and eradicate any bad habits you might fall into, and you will be fully equipped to develop your own style of presenting with flair.

And when you feel confident that you can deliver any speech, in any venue, to any audience, you should begin to really enjoy public speaking, too.

Dynamic expression and presentation

> *'Acting should be bigger than life. Scripts should be bigger than life. It should all be bigger than life.'*
>
> Bette Davis, US actress

Even the best speech can be marred by an uninspiring speech-giver; indeed, it can actually be difficult to listen for any length of time to someone whose presentation is flat and monotone. Furthermore, if the speaker appears to lack interest in their own material, why should their audience be any different? By injecting some energy and passion into your speech, and by mastering the techniques for dynamic expression and presentation, you can ensure that your speech receives the attention it deserves from your audience.

The techniques outlined in this chapter will enable you to deliver your speech in a manner which is:

● engaging
● sincere
● passionate
● inspirational
● memorable.

Remember that no one technique alone will suffice – it is the combination of methods and approaches which will elevate your speech-giving.

Make sure that you practise your speech early – and often – to discover the combination of techniques which:

● best suits your style
● allows you to achieve the desired tone
● best communicates your message
● makes you feel most comfortable and confident
● will most appeal to, and suit, your audience.

SUNDAY
MONDAY
TUESDAY
WEDNESDAY
THURSDAY
FRIDAY
SATURDAY

TIP *Experiment with different combinations of techniques until you find your preferred style. Remember that you can also use these techniques to tailor your delivery for every speech you make, and for every audience.*

Effective use of pauses and phrasing

'It's not so much knowing when to speak as when to pause.'

Jack Benny, US comedian

A much overlooked aspect of public speaking is knowing when *not* to speak. Just as someone talking too quickly is difficult, and tiring, to listen to, and their message is often lost as a result, so someone talking without pausing runs the very real risk of having their audience tune them out and switch off.

Effective use of pauses, on the other hand, helps to break up the pattern of your speech so that it's pleasingly phrased, doesn't run into one never-ending sentence, and is easily absorbed. Pauses will also:

- allow your audience to take in what you have said
- give your audience time to digest your message
- build anticipation and expectation of what you will say
- break up any long sections into manageable chunks
- prevent you from gabbling, and your speech from running away from you
- allow you to prepare for the next part of your speech.

TIP *If you wish to inject some humour into your speech, try using a 'pregnant pause' – pausing at the end of a phrase to build suspense before a punch line.*

Varying your pace, pitch and volume

Pace

Varying the pace of your delivery helps to maintain your audience's interest. It can also help to underline what you're saying.

Speaking **slowly** is ideal when:

- you are saying something serious
- you need to be solemn
- you want to add extra gravity to your message
- what you are saying is complex.

Speaking **quickly** is ideal when:

- you want to keep your message light
- what you are saying will be familiar to your audience
- you are using humour
- you are saying something upbeat.

TIP *Whatever pace you are aiming for, the temptation is to rush – particularly if you are nervous. So remember to go more slowly than you think you should. A good rule of thumb is to halve the speed you think feels right, and halve it again if you are nervous.*

Remember that it's important to keep to the appropriate pace for what you are saying, but that any pace will become boring if it's maintained for too long. Varying your pace is key.

Pitch

Another way to help to convey your message effectively is to vary the pitch of your voice according to the content of your speech and the effect you are hoping to have.

Use a **low** pitch to help convey:

- seriousness
- solemnity
- genuineness.

Use a **high** pitch to help convey:

- lightness
- humour
- excitement.

As with pace, varying the pitch of your voice will help to keep your audience interested and engaged, and will also help you to best convey your message. Combining different speeds of delivery with different vocal pitches can really help to generate different feels to your speech, so practise to find out which are most useful to you, and most appropriate for your speech.

 The exact pitch of your voice will depend on whether your voice is naturally deep (low pitch) or naturally light (high pitch). Being aware of this will help to prevent you from delivering your speech with an unwanted vocal message.

Volume

Often people are under the misconception that volume is something they won't need to concern themselves with, particularly if they will be presenting to a small group in an enclosed space, or if they will be using a microphone. In fact, effective use of volume is just as important as effective use of pace and pitch, and once again the key is to use it to add variety – speaking at just one level for your entire speech can quickly have a soporific effect!

Keeping your voice varied and interesting

The need to vary your volume is especially acute if your voice is naturally very low, or devoid of cadence. Injecting variety into the volume of your delivery can be a great way to prevent any monotone creeping into your speech patterns, and to ensure that your voice is interesting to listen to over a sustained period.

Dropping your voice can have the effect of making your audience listen harder to what you're saying and can help to give emphasis as a result; equally, raising your voice can have the effect of driving home your message. These techniques can be employed (and can be just as effective) whether or not your voice will be amplified, but be careful not to overuse them.

Effective use of vocal tone and inflection

Vocal tone

The tone of your voice is the underlying message implicit in what you are saying – regardless of the content. It's therefore vitally important to be aware of the tone since it can convey an unwanted or unintended sentiment. By learning to use it to your advantage, however, you can colour your voice with meaning, emotion and feelings, such as:

● sincerity
● gravitas
● pride
● fear
● excitement
● warmth
● humour.

This will enable you to convey the appropriate sentiment quickly and openly, and it will actively support your message.

Identify the primary sentiment for each section of your speech and determine how you will achieve it – then highlight it in your notes.

Inflection

The inflection in your voice means the rising and falling patterns you create in your speech. This is important to:

● help paint a picture of what you're saying
● introduce vocal variety
● keep your audience interested
● underline the most important parts.

By modulating your voice you can help to ensure your manner of speaking is interesting to listen to, and that the content of your speech is delivered with maximum impact.

TIP *Avoid the dreaded 'rising inflection'! Unless you are asking a question, you should always make sure that you bring your voice down at the end of a sentence. (Unless you're from the Antipodes!)*

Appropriate use of audio-visual and multi-media materials and props

The key word here is 'appropriate'. Many a speech is marred by inappropriate use of these tools, most commonly through overuse. This is usually because the speaker:

● wants to use them as a distraction to take the focus off themselves
● is unconfident in their material or their ability to deliver it
● feels that using these tools makes their speech seem more 'professional'
● feels that using these tools validates their material
● feels that it's required of them, a necessary part of every good speech
● thinks it will give them a nice break!

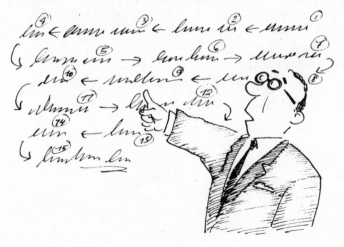

Think about it from the audience's point of view, though – if they are presented with a series of slides, a PowerPoint presentation or a video clip and cannot immediately see its relevance and why you are using it, it will set off alarm bells for them over the quality of your speech.

Put simply, these tools are often used as an excuse for not having great material or for the inability to deliver it well, and this is easily spotted by an astute audience. They should therefore be avoided unless you have a very good reason to use them, and if you do you must know exactly why it's better to communicate your material in this way rather than delivering it though your speech.

So what constitutes appropriate and inappropriate use?

Appropriate use

- showing video clips of people giving their opinions on a subject, first-hand
- showing photographs which would be difficult to describe
- succinctly communicating a lot of data – but only if the data really needs to be shown
- displaying objects which are best seen 'in the flesh'
- giving your audience a breather.

Inappropriate use

- demonstrating anything which could be better presented through your speech
- use of data-rich presentations which are:
  - unnecessary
  - difficult for your audience to take in
  - better presented as handouts for later consumption
- any form of overuse
- time-fillers
- giving yourself a breather.

 TIP *A good rule of thumb is to ensure that anything which you elect to communicate in this way cannot be better communicated in a different way, and particularly through your speech, and that you're using these tools for the benefit of the audience and not yourself.*

Overcoming mistakes

'Do not fear mistakes. You will know failure. Continue to reach out.'

Benjamin Franklin, US Founding Father

If standing in front of a large group of people and speaking is something you don't do on a regular basis, it's highly probable that you will make a mistake (or several!). That doesn't matter – what matters is how you deal with them. Remember that everyone makes 'mistakes', even when speaking casually to friends in a relaxed environment.

How often have you found yourself with a frog in your throat, or mispronouncing something, or that a word or phrase came out differently from the way you had intended? It happens to everyone and it's no big deal – but when you're standing in front of a group of people, and the whole point of what you are doing is speaking, it can suddenly take on huge significance.

Try thinking of it from the audience's point of view though – or from your point of view if you were a member of the audience. If you heard a speaker make a mistake, would you mind? Would you think less of them for stumbling over a word or momentarily losing their place in their speech? Of course, you wouldn't. What you would care about is how they dealt with it. If they seem to go to pieces, or are terribly embarrassed or apologetic, or as a consequence rush through the rest of their speech, you may quickly begin to lose confidence in them as a speaker – even though you might empathize with them and be glad that it's them and not you in that situation!

If, on the other hand, they quickly and calmly get themselves back on track you will admire them for it, and here's the really interesting thing – you will admire them more because of it. So making a mistake is not always a bad thing, provided you deal with it well.

The key to dealing with mistakes is to have thought through as many of them as possible in advance, and know how you will deal with them if and when they occur. Study the table below.

Common mistakes	How to overcome them
Stumbling over words	Just repeat them, more slowly. Remember to take your time – the audience will be happy to wait and you need to ensure that you don't stumble over your words repeatedly.
Losing your place in the 'script'	Take your time to find it again. Your notes should be clearly labelled and numbered, so finding your place shouldn't be difficult or take long – but the more you try to rush, the harder it will be. Remember: 'More haste, less speed.'
Never lifting your head	Make regular eye contact. If you realize after a while that you haven't been making regular eye contact with your audience, just begin to do so from that point. It can feel strange to suddenly begin to do this partway through your speech, but it's much better than not doing it at all.
Speaking too quietly	Deliver every word to the back of the room. This is easier if you are using a microphone but even then the levels may not have been set up for you, so you may find you still need to be aware of delivering your words loudly, clearly and with confidence.
Panicking	Take a deep breath and carry on. It's not uncommon for a speaker to panic, and usually the horrible feeling of panic rising through your body, constricting your throat and flooding you with fear, quickly passes. Taking a deep, slow breath can help, as can taking a sip of water. Then just carry on, remembering not to rush.
Fidgeting	Stand still and tall, and keep your hands occupied. Remember that fidgeting is a sure giveaway that you are nervous, and it's distracting to your audience and makes them concerned about your ability to deliver. Concentrate on standing still and keeping your hands on your notes or on the lectern.

By knowing how you will act if the situation arises, you can prepare yourself for how you will react; and by preparing yourself thoroughly for what you will do in each situation, you will give yourself every chance of dealing with it in a professional manner. Even if something completely unexpected happens, by preparing yourself to deal with the unexpected you will have put yourself in a position to deal with it calmly and confidently.

Eliminating bad habits

Every speaker, whether seasoned or new to speech-giving, will need to be mindful of the likelihood that they will develop bad habits with regards to their public-speaking technique. The best way to keep on top of this, and to remedy it as and when it occurs, is to ask a colleague to watch you every so often and to give you honest feedback. Some points for them to consider include:

- Have you started to rush your words?
- Have you developed any distracting fidgeting?
- Are you shuffling your feet?
- Are you audible?
- Are you gabbling?
- Are you making eye contact with your audience?
- Do you look nervous?
- Are your speech and your message coming across clearly?

It is possible to keep an eye on these things yourself, but it really is much better having someone do it for you since they will be devoting all their efforts to it, and not trying to give a good speech at the same time! Many a speaker has come unstuck during the course of giving their speech because they were trying to evaluate themselves as they gave it. Also, an 'outside eye' is better placed to notice bad habits.

Impress!

As a starting point, ask the person assessing you whether you 'IMPRESS' them as you speak:

Inflection – is your speech being delivered with interesting vocal variety?

Movement – are you guilty of shuffling your feet or fidgeting?

Pause – is your speech broken up with appropriate pauses, or are you rushing through it?

Reach the back of the room – is your speech audible, both in terms of volume and clarity?

Eye contact – are you lifting your head from your notes and taking in your audience?

Stand tall – do you look interested and alert? Does your body language convey the right impression?

Speak slowly – are you taking your time and getting your message across or are you gabbling?

By combining and employing these advanced techniques, you will soon develop a style which really works for you. As you gain in confidence, try pushing the techniques further and further – then rein them back in to their most productive point for you. With regular practice you will soon be able to master the art of successful, dynamic public speaking.

Summary

Once you have mastered the basics of public speaking, it's time to practise the more advanced techniques, the successful employment of which will elevate your speech from simply 'good' to 'outstanding'. By learning the principles of using your voice and face to put your speech across to your audience in a way which is engaging and memorable, you will be able to create and deliver speeches which people will look forward to hearing, and talk positively about long after.

And by learning how to identify and get rid of your bad habits, and how to pre-empt and overcome any mistakes which might occur, you will put yourself in the enviable position of being able to do full justice to every speech you give.

We are now almost halfway through the week, so tomorrow we will consider how you can maximize the impact of your speech...

SUNDAY

MONDAY

TUESDAY

WEDNESDAY

THURSDAY

FRIDAY

SATURDAY

Fact-check [answers at the back]

1. It's best to use a combination of presentation techniques because...
   a) You spread your chances of using a good one ❏
   b) Each one is rubbish on its own ❏
   c) The audience might not understand some of them ❏
   d) This will allow you to achieve the desired tone and style ❏

2. Effective use of pauses will...
   a) Build anticipation and expectation of what you will say ❏
   b) Spin out your speech so you don't need to write much ❏
   c) Create convenient snack breaks for you ❏
   d) Fool the audience into thinking you have forgotten what comes next ❏

3. Varying the pace of your delivery helps to...
   a) Confuse the audience ❏
   b) Unsettle the audience ❏
   c) Maintain your audience's interest ❏
   d) Stop the audience from going to sleep ❏

4. Using the appropriate vocal pitch and volume will...
   a) Pre-empt what is coming ❏
   b) Keep the audience engaged and help to underline your message ❏
   c) Confuse the audience ❏
   d) Quickly become boring to listen to ❏

5. The tone of your voice is...
   a) Crucial to the speed at which you convey information ❏
   b) Best when it's patronizing or condescending ❏
   c) The underlying message implicit in what you are saying – regardless of the content ❏
   d) Impossible to regulate in cold conditions ❏

6. A mastery of vocal inflection will help you to...
   a) Become more supple over time ❏
   b) Swallow large food items without risk of choking ❏
   c) Bend reverentially on one knee ❏
   d) Paint a picture of what you are saying ❏

7. A common reason for the overuse of audio-visual and multi-media materials and props is...
   a) You have got lots so you might as well use them ❏
   b) Wanting to use them as a distraction to take the focus off yourself ❏
   c) You might disappoint technology fans if you don't ❏
   d) Everyone loves a puppet show ❏

8. You are likely to make some mistakes when speaking in public because...
   a) You are rubbish ❏
   b) You refuse to practise and love to 'wing it' on the day ❏
   c) Everyone does – no matter how good they are ❏
   d) People will be heckling ❏

9. If you do make a mistake...
a) There is nothing you can do ❏
b) You should give an immediate, heartfelt apology ❏
c) It's best to stop there and then ❏
d) It doesn't matter – just carry on ❏

10. You are likely to develop some bad habits over time because...
a) You are careless ❏
b) It's a natural effect of repeating any action ❏
c) You are naturally slipshod in your work ❏
d) It's peculiar to public speaking but happens to everyone ❏

SUNDAY

MONDAY

TUESDAY

WEDNESDAY

THURSDAY

FRIDAY

SATURDAY

WEDNESDAY

Delivering your speech with maximum impact

Now that you have learned how to write a great speech, and learned the techniques of public speaking, it's time to learn how to deliver your speech with maximum impact, in order to create the maximum effect.

You have the necessary tools at your disposal but putting them into practice requires a new set of skills. Imagine someone being trained to be a soldier – getting fit and learning how to use a weapon are necessary skills, but putting them into practice on a battlefield is something else altogether. The tools and techniques outlined in the previous chapters will have provided you with a valuable new skill set – now it's time to learn how to employ those skills to transform your speech-giving from competent to truly memorable.

Today you will learn how to command the space from start to finish, to engage with your audience, to look confident (despite how you might be feeling!), and to deliver your speech with dynamism and élan. But we will also look at some of the practical issues such as getting to know the venue (whether or not you are able to visit it in person) and preparing for unexpected eventualities.

Checking out the venue

If possible, it's a great idea to scope out the venue in advance. Getting the 'lie of the land' will help you in a number of ways:

● Seeing the venue, and where you will stand to give your speech, will help to settle your nerves.
● You will be able to determine the size of the space, and whether or not you will need (and be able to have) amplification.
● You will be able to determine how far you may have to walk to get to the podium from your seat – and how long that will take.
● You will be able to see whether there are any 'hidden' surprises.

It's particularly valuable to check out the venue if you are nervous about giving your speech. There will be enough pressure on you on the day without adding any surprises or unwelcome complications, and most venues are happy to let people visit to orient themselves within the space where they will be giving their speech.

It's amazing what a difference it makes to how you will feel on the day if you can enter a space you already know. If you know where everything is, where you will be speaking from, how far away the audience will be, the acoustics, and so on, you will feel exponentially more relaxed about giving your speech. You will also have the advantage of it feeling like 'home' to you, while it's unfamiliar to everyone else. See whether you can practise your speech while you are there – a dry run *in situ* is a wonderful confidence boost.

Other ways of learning about the venue

If you're unable to visit the venue in person before the day, you may be able to see photos or even a video clip of it online. Some venues provide this on their website, while you may be able to find footage of people giving a speech in the venue on popular sharing sites such as YouTube.

Failing this, you may know someone who has been there, or else call the venue with a set of questions which will

help to give you the 'lie of the land' in advance. In the
worst-case scenario, where none of this is possible, ensure that you arrive at the venue extra early to give yourself time to orient yourself and to begin to feel familiar
with the space.

Making sure that you're heard

When it comes to listening to speeches, there is little more
aggravating than not being able to hear the speaker – and from
the speaker's point of view, there is nothing more aggravating
than working hard to give a great speech only for it not be
heard. Most venues will have checked the sound levels and
provided amplification if necessary but this is not always the
case, so make sure that you arrive early and take the time to
ensure that your speech gets heard.

If you're going to use a **microphone** you will need to learn
how to use it properly, and even if you feel you don't need
one because you have a loud voice, unless the venue is
really intimate it's usually best to use a microphone. This will:

● take the pressure off you having to project
● make you sound more relaxed, confident and in control
● allow more vocal expression and subtlety
● allow you to continue over any interruptions!

*If you have a particularly soft or quiet voice, you may
find that you need to use a microphone when other
people don't. This may not be provided automatically
by the venue. Contact them in advance and request a
microphone be made available. That way, if you find you
don't need it, it doesn't matter – but, if you do, it will be
there waiting for you.*

Fortunately, there is no great mystery to using a microphone
effectively, and even if you have never used one before and
do not have time to practise with it before giving your speech
it shouldn't present too many problems, provided that you
remember the basic principles given in the table below:

How to hold it	Hold it in a comfortable, open fist, ensuring that you don't obscure the mesh. Try to keep it vertical so that you are speaking across the top of it.
Where to hold it	The top of the microphone should be just in front of your chin.
How to speak into it	Speak normally, keeping your voice at a constant volume, and be careful not to breathe loudly as this can be picked up by the microphone.

The seven giveaways of a nervous speaker

Controlling your nerves is important, and we will look at this as a separate topic in Friday's chapter, but it's also important that you don't *look* nervous. Appearances count for a lot when you are speaking in public – if you can get the audience to relax and believe in you as a good speaker, then you are already halfway there. Creating a good impression is vital – you will want to look calm, confident and in control.

Several things, however, can undermine this. These are some of the most common giveaways you will want to avoid:

- fidgeting
- rapid swallowing
- frequent coughing
- nervous laughter
- not lifting your head up
- avoiding eye contact
- speaking too quickly.

 If you appear nervous, your audience will be nervous – which in turn will make you even more nervous! If you appear calm and confident, your audience will relax – and so will you.

Keeping the audience on your side

By applying the techniques we have looked at, you can get the audience on your side and feeling relaxed from the outset, so their expectation will be of an interesting, engaging and enjoyable speech.

In many ways, that's the hard part done – what you have to do now is to keep it going. To do so there are some key points to remember:

- Keep smiling – even if you feel it's going badly!
- Make eye contact with as many people as possible.
- Remember not to fidget, or shuffle your feet.
- Don't be tempted to rush – take your time and let your audience soak up and appreciate your speech.
- Keep to the script – this will ensure that your material is first-rate.
- Try to ensure that you sound like you are confident and enjoying yourself.

TIP *There is no reason to suppose that your audience will be hoping you fail – so give them 'permission' to relax by appearing confident and in control at all times.*

Engaging with the audience from start to finish

A bored speaker is a boring speaker. It's hard work and off-putting listening to someone who seems uninterested in their material, or who gives the impression that they don't really want to be giving their speech at all. On the other hand, listening to someone who seems genuinely interested in their material, and who gives the impression that they genuinely want to communicate it, can be energizing and inspiring; there is also a much greater chance that you will remember what you have heard.

So, engaging with your audience right from the word go, and continuing to do so throughout your speech, is crucial to ensuring that your message is heard and that your audience is stimulated. We have looked at ways of achieving this but it's worth looking at some of the pitfalls and pratfalls which can get in the way and undermine your hard work.

Reason for lack of engagement	Solution
Lack of ownership	If you haven't written the speech yourself, or have written only a part of it, you may not feel that you have much invested interest. If you feel disconnected from your speech, then so will your audience, so you will need to find a way to include only material for which you can feel real ownership.
Heard it so many times before	If you are to give a speech you are used to giving, there is a real danger of it coming across as flat and uninspiring. Worse still, you may give the impression that even you are bored with it! You will need to be mindful of the fact that your audience will be hearing it for the first time – so you need to deliver it as though you are doing so for the first time, too!
Don't believe in what you are saying	In a worst-case scenario, you may be giving a speech which includes material you disagree with. Sometimes this is unavoidable, such as when you are giving a speech on behalf of a company and need to reflect the views of a number of stakeholders. You will need to remember that for those people the material is accurate and important, and that is how it must be delivered. Never be tempted to use the speech-giving as an opportunity to make known your opinion of their views. You will need to ensure that you have ownership of this material, so try to ensure that you fully understand their point of view.
Hate giving speeches	Giving speeches may be a highlight of your working year. For many people, however, it's a worry or a chore rather than a delight. If this is the case for you, you will need to be mindful of the reason why you are giving it, of its importance to you and to your company, and of the audience members who are giving up their time to hear it. Then dig deep, remember the techniques for dealing with nerves and appearing confident, and try to enjoy your speech-giving as much as possible.
Need to be doing something else	The time pressure of modern working life often means that we feel that we really don't have the time to attend conferences, or give speeches. If this is the case for you, you will need to be clear about your priorities and commit to giving speeches only when you have the time and desire to do so fully. If you have no choice but to give a speech, even when you don't have the time, you will need to understand why this is being prioritized by your bosses, and then concentrate fully on giving the speech well and resolving any conflicts later on.

Varying your delivery

Imagine driving across a vast desert, with nothing to break the journey, no stops, and no interesting scenery along the way. You would soon be bored, and shortly after that you would mentally switch off, driving on autopilot and subconsciously waiting for the journey to end. This is what it's like listening to a dull speaker, someone who talks in a flat monotone, who doesn't break up their speech, and who doesn't use any of the tools and techniques for injecting variety into their delivery.

By using your voice to paint a picture of what you're saying for your audience, and by using your facial expression and body language to communicate your interest in, and passion for, your subject, you will be able to hook the audience and keep them interested. And by adding vocal variety to your delivery you will be able to take them on a journey which is enjoyable and stimulating.

Using the actor's method of projection and voice control

One of the fundamentals of acting, which every student of the theatre is required to learn before they can progress, is voice control. If an actor can't be heard, and heard clearly, then it really doesn't matter how good their acting is, it will just be wasted. The same is true of speech-givers, and so the same consideration must be given to mastering voice control.

It's likely that you will be using a microphone if the venue in which you are giving your speech is large, so it's not so important to conquer the more advanced techniques of what is known as 'bellows breathing', diaphragm control and supporting your voice for clear projection – but control of your voice is crucial. This is because it will allow you the flexibility to deliver your speech in exactly the way you want to, the way which you know will best put it across. You won't be restricted by limitations on what you can do with your voice, which might otherwise hamper your delivery.

The best way to achieve complete control of your voice, and at the same time increase its vocal range to enhance the scope of techniques in your armoury, is to practise vocal exercises. There are a great many of these, and details of a wide range can be found on the Internet, but to get you started here are a few of the most fundamental:

Exercise	What to do	How it helps
Yawning	Yawn, stretching your mouth as wide as possible, and vocalize as you exhale.	This is one of the best exercises for expanding and relaxing your throat, vital for the creation of a clear, pure, unconstricted sound.
Tongue stretches	Open your mouth wide, and stick out your tongue as far as it will go. Then try to touch your nose, your chin and each ear with it, in turn. Then use your tongue to describe a large circle.	These will help you to improve the mobility and the strength of your tongue – the primary organ of articulation.
Deep breathing	Stand with your feet shoulder-width apart and relax. Breathe in through your nose and inhale a really big lungful, concentrating on feeling your chest expand. Hold it for a few seconds and exhale slowly through your mouth.	This will help you to relax, and will encourage your lungs to take in more air, allowing you to better support your voice.
Vocalizing your breathing	As above but begin the exhalation as a gentle hum, and try to feel it tickling your lips. Gradually increase the volume of the hum and then open your mouth and allow the sound out as an extended 'aaahh'. Hold the note for as long as you can.	This is a great way to practise generating a clear, true sound, and to train your vocal muscles and responses to work properly to allow the sound to travel undisturbed from your body to your audience's ears. It also helps in the development of the intercostal muscles, important for breath control.
Shoulder rolls	Stand with your feet shoulder-width apart and relax. Lift your shoulders up towards your ears, then back to neutral, then push them down as far as they will go. Back to neutral before pushing	Tightness in the shoulders is a sure-fire way to create tension in your body, and this will lead to a tightness in your voice. This exercise, practised regularly, will help to increase

	them forwards and backwards, and finally describing large circles with them.	the range of motion in your shoulders, and your ability to keep them relaxed.
Jaw extensions	Stand with your feet shoulder width apart and relax. Allow your jaw to relax so that it drops slightly, then swing it gently from side to side.	Any tension in your jaw will adversely affect your ability to deliver your speech since it tightens your mouth, making proper articulation difficult to achieve.

TIP *Try timing yourself on the 'Vocalizing your breathing' exercise. Start from the moment you exhale (as humming) and continue through the open mouth exhalation until you run out of breath. Over time you should be able to reach 30 seconds or more. Try to make sure that you keep your mouth really wide open and your throat relaxed, so that the sound produced is clear and unimpeded.*

Commanding the space

This is predominantly a matter of confidence – not of *feeling* confident, but of *looking* confident. As long as your audience thinks you are confident they will relax and be more receptive to your speech. Commanding the space, then, is an important factor in establishing the framework for a successful speech. The following techniques will help you to accomplish it:

- Walk confidently and with purpose to the podium.
- Lift your head and take in the audience.
- Smile, and look relaxed.
- Breathe deeply, and slowly, and support your voice for a strong, clear delivery.
- Stand still and avoid fidgeting.
- Speak slowly and clearly.
- Make eye contact with your audience throughout your speech.

Remember the three Cs: by following these simple steps you can appear calm, confident and in control, allowing you to command the space.

Essential preparation

By getting yourself prepared well in advance, both practically and psychologically, you will feel more confident about your speech-giving. In addition to visiting the venue and practising your speech *in situ*, you will need to prepare your cue cards, together with any additional physical material such as slides or props – as well as thinking through as many potentially speech-ruining eventualities as possible and ways to deal with them. This will help you to relax and to deliver your speech to the very best of your ability.

If you will be using **props**, it's best to prepare these as soon as possible. Doing so will give you time to:

- practise with them
- make sure you know how they work
- work them seamlessly into your delivery
- make sure you can get all the items you need.

If you are using **technical** items (sound, lighting, slides, etc.), be sure to check:

- that there will be a power outlet to hand
- whether they require time to warm-up
- that you have a backup plan if they fail to work!

SUNDAY
MONDAY
TUESDAY
WEDNESDAY
THURSDAY
FRIDAY
SATURDAY

Remember that using these extra elements can help to break up your speech and add interest but they should never be the mainstay – a ratio of 80–90 per cent speech to 10–20 per cent additional elements is a good rule of thumb.

Stepping stones

For your speech to be really well received, and long remembered, it's crucial that your delivery is first-rate. As a useful checklist for delivering your speech with dynamism, use the 'STEPPING STONES' acronym:

Smile – nothing says you are confident of giving a great speech as quickly as the appearance that you are calm, in control and looking forward to giving it – and a relaxed smile does just that.

Tone – establishing the desired tone early on is a great way of managing the audience's expectations, and conveying the subtext of your speech.

Energy – no one likes to be faced with a lifeless speaker. Do a good warm-up before you start, and attack your speech with verve, enthusiasm and lots of energy.

Pace – remember not to rush. Your audience will need time to take in, and soak up, what you are saying.

Pause – this will help to emphasize the most important parts of your speech, and give your audience the opportunity to properly digest it.

Inflection – injecting vocal variety into your speech is crucial to ensure that it's pleasant to listen to, and easy to remember.

Nerves – getting your nerves under control, and even using them to your advantage, can really help to give you the edge in making a great speech.

Give out the right attitude – the audience will respond well if you appear calm, confident and collected, and enthusiastic about your subject and the opportunity to talk about it.

Style – try to make sure that nothing you say or do, or the way in which it's said or done, is ever bland. Think through each part of your speech to see how you can add style and interest.

Try not to fidget – there are few things more off-putting to the audience than distracting fidgeting, so make sure that you have identified your weaknesses in this area and work to eliminate them.

Observe the audience – monitoring the audience is a great way of making sure that you are on track and that they are keeping up; adjust your delivery accordingly.

No distractions – stay focused on your delivery and ensure that you have eliminated any obvious potential distractions (e.g. turning off your mobile phone or pager, and reminding the audience to do likewise).

Energy and enthusiasm – give out lots of energy and your audience will feed off it and respond accordingly. Similarly, if you are enthusiastic about your subject, so will your audience be.

Say it with confidence – with everything in place you have every reason to feel confident that you will deliver a truly memorable speech.

Summary

No matter how good you become at writing a great speech, and no matter how accomplished you are at each of the public-speaking techniques we have looked at, if you can't deliver your speech with maximum impact then all the rest will have served little or no purpose. Delivering your speech with dynamism and flair is crucial to first-rate public speaking. By mastering the techniques of getting – and keeping – the audience on your side, and of commanding the space while delivering your speech with vocal variety and ensuring that you are heard, you will be well on your way to becoming on orator of some distinction.

By visiting the venue in advance, where possible, or at least researching it as thoroughly as you can, you will be prepared for what lies ahead and can begin to plan accordingly. Better still, try out your speech *in situ*.

Tomorrow we will be looking at how best to practise your speech.

SUNDAY
MONDAY
TUESDAY
WEDNESDAY
THURSDAY
FRIDAY
SATURDAY

Fact-check [answers at the back]

1. Checking out the venue in advance is useful because...
   a) It will help to settle your nerves ❏
   b) You will know where it is ❏
   c) You will know where the toilets are ❏
   d) You can find the nearest exit for a quick escape ❏

2. Practising your speech in the venue is a good idea because...
   a) You can leave prompts around the room ❏
   b) It will help to settle your nerves ❏
   c) You will know if you can see over the lectern ❏
   d) People will be fed up of you practising it elsewhere ❏

3. You should always arrive early and check the sound levels because...
   a) The venue's last use may have been as a disco ❏
   b) You do not know how loud your voice is ❏
   c) You can take the appropriate steps to ensure that your speech can be heard ❏
   d) You will know if you should have brought a microphone ❏

4. Unless the venue is really small, it's a good idea to use a microphone because...
   a) It will save you having to project, allowing more vocal expression and subtlety ❏
   b) It makes you look more professional ❏
   c) It prevents you from fidgeting with your hands ❏
   d) It allows you to sing as well as to speak ❏

5. Appearances count for a lot when you are speaking in public because...
   a) They take attention away from what you are saying ❏
   b) Looking professional and confident helps the audience to relax and to believe in you ❏
   c) If you look good, no one will care how good your speech is ❏
   d) You might go on somewhere nice afterwards ❏

6. It's important to start confidently and to set an appropriate tone because...
   a) Even if it all goes horribly wrong, at least you started well ❏
   b) Otherwise the audience may not know what you are talking about ❏
   c) You can fool some of the people all of the time ❏
   d) It settles the audience and improves their perception of you ❏

7. It's important that you are interested in your material because...
a) It will help to prevent you from dozing off ❏
b) A bored speaker is a boring speaker ❏
c) Otherwise you may be tempted to talk about something else altogether ❏
d) No one else will be ❏

8. It can be useful to employ the actors' method of projection and voice control when...
a) There is no amplification available ❏
b) You start to become sleepy ❏
c) You start to become bored ❏
d) You decide you would rather be an actor ❏

9. It's important to talk slowly and clearly because...
a) Some of your audience may be hard of hearing ❏
b) People may want to take notes ❏
c) It allows you to confidently command the space ❏
d) Some of your audience may be foreign ❏

10. You can feel more confident about your speech-giving by...
a) Getting yourself prepared well in advance, practically and psychologically ❏
b) Having triplicates of all your notes ❏
c) Having it all recorded and mouthing to the soundtrack ❏
d) Getting someone else to do it for you ❏

THURSDAY

Practising your speech

How often have you heard it said that 'Practice makes perfect'? And yet it's amazing how many people think that simply writing their speech is sufficient preparation for giving it! If you're unused to public speaking, it's especially important to familiarize yourself with your speech, and the way in which you intend to deliver it, in order to give yourself the best possible chance of success.

Speech-giving is a skill which needs to learned, and then practised, just like any other skill – and you shouldn't expect it to come quickly or feel natural straight away. You wouldn't expect to be able to drive a car the first time you sat behind the wheel, no matter how much you had read about the process. You would know that practical experience is the only way to master the skill – and that it takes time, repetition and hard work. It's exactly the same with learning to give a great speech.

By practising your speech, you will grow in confidence while honing your technique to ensure that you deliver it to the very best of your ability. Don't feel that you need to wait until your speech is finished to start practising either – the sooner you start the better; and the more practice you put in, particularly in front of a few people, the more confident you will become.

Practice makes perfect

Delivering a speech well is a skill which needs to be learned and practised. How much practice you will need to put in will depend on a number of factors, including:

- previous experience
- natural aptitude
- level of confidence.

However, no matter what your starting position, the more practice you put in the better your speech will be. So, practise early and practise often.

Saying it out loud

Remember that one of the things which often throws people when they are unused to giving speeches is hearing the sound of their own voice out loud – if you're not used to public speaking, you will be amazed how odd this sounds at first! Most people are rarely conscious of hearing their own voice in everyday situations, but when it's the only sound in the room and everyone is listening to you, you will hear it in a whole new light – and it's something you need to get used to.

Fortunately, it's something which can be practised any time you're on your own, for example when driving your car or while doing the housework. It doesn't matter what you say: just get used to speaking out loud, and loudly. If you find it difficult to think of things to say, try listening to an all-talk radio station and simply repeating whatever is being said.

By giving yourself the opportunity to get used to hearing your own voice (and one which forces you to concentrate on it), you will quickly become comfortable with it, and even make it seem normal.

There will be enough things to contend with when you are standing in front of an audience to give your speech, without adding to them by being startled at the sound of your own voice. Worse still, if you are, it will almost certainly make you self-conscious, so get used to it early. Bear in mind that, if your speech is recorded, your voice on playback will sound very different from the way it sounds in your head – another reason people become overly self-aware. Remember, though, that this is the way it sounds to everyone else all the time – for them the shock would be if they heard your voice the way you hear it.

TIP *Repetition through practice will not only improve your delivery but also enable you to better control your nerves.*

Gaining in confidence

> *'How often in life we complete a task that was beyond the capability of the person we were when we started it.'*
>
> Robert Brault, US writer

As you practise, your confidence level increases to a directly proportionate degree. So the more you put in the more you get out. And the tougher you make your 'training', the bigger the rewards will be, and the easier it will be to give your speech on the day.

As you gain in confidence you will:

- start to feel more relaxed
- start to look more relaxed
- slow down your delivery
- make more eye contact with your audience
- make better use of pauses
- add more variety to your delivery
- control your fidgeting
- begin to actually enjoy giving your speech!

Using a mirror to highlight bad habits

*'The world more often rewards the
appearance of merit than merit itself.'*

François de La Rochefoucauld, French writer of maxims

Looking as though you know what you are doing is half the battle.
Appearances can be deceptive, and you can use this to your
advantage if you don't feel confident. Remember that projecting
a positive image will help your audience to relax – which will help
you to relax.

One of the best ways to monitor your appearance is to use
a mirror, preferably one which is full-length. This really is an
invaluable tool in helping you to get used to standing tall, and
still, and looking confident. It will also highlight any bad habits
you may have, or which creep in over time, so try to get into the
habit of practising in front of a mirror on a regular basis.

 *Smaller mirrors can be angled to focus on different areas
in turn, for example face, hands and feet.*

Practise delivering part of your speech, paying particular attention to whether you:

- stand up tall
- shuffle your feet
- fidget
- shift your weight from one leg to the other
- play with your hands
- breathe more rapidly, or less deeply
- feel self-conscious.

By observing and monitoring your appearance you can help to eradicate any distracting habits you may have while building your confidence and losing your inhibitions.

Rehearsing in front of other people

The next step on from practising in front of a mirror (or perhaps filming yourself) is to practise in front of other people – rehearsing your speech in front of an audience is vital preparation for any speech-giver. You can start with just one person and build up to a few people, such as colleagues, family members or close friends. Initially, you are likely to feel:

- nervous
- awkward
- embarrassed
- self-conscious.

This is entirely natural but will subside with practice and experience, leaving you free to concentrate on presenting your material with passion and dynamism, and – I hope – to enjoy doing so. You will find it all but impossible to give of your best if you cannot relax, and all but impossible to relax if the first time you give your speech in front of an audience is when you give your speech on the day. Remember that, however bad going through this process makes you feel, it's far better to get past this hurdle now than to face it for the first time when you actually stand up to present your speech for real.

There is no substitute for practice and the more often you can practise in front of other people the better you will get. Practising in front of other people has the additional bonus that you are able to receive constructive criticism from them. Make sure that you ask them for this in advance so that they know you want to hear what they think, and ask them to be completely honest – no matter how much you may not like hearing what they have to say, it's better to hear it from them than from members of the audience on the day when it's too late to do anything about it.

Try using different people as your 'practice audience', when possible, so that:

- you don't become too familiar with them
- they don't become too familiar with your speech
- you receive the widest possible range of feedback.

Projecting a positive image, and the need to exude confidence

When you stand up to make your speech the audience becomes *your* audience. First impressions are critical, and the secret is that, no matter how you feel inside, the audience will perceive only what you project to them. Think of yourself as an actor, and the person who will be giving your speech as a character. Think of the characteristics you would want them to have as well as those characteristics you wouldn't want them to have:

✓ confident	✗ nervous
✓ in control	✗ dreading having to give the speech
✓ pleased to be there	✗ worried they are going to make a fool of themselves
✓ looking forward to giving the speech	✗ impatient to get it over with

> ### *'I'm no good at public speaking, but if I can assume a role and speak as that person, then I'm fine.'*
> Jason Wiles, US actor

By thinking of yourself as an actor playing a character you can help to distance yourself from the real you, the person who may be unconfident, unused to speech-giving, or nervous. You can then decide what impression you want your audience to have of you, and create exactly that. Appearances can be deceptive – so use that to your advantage.

TIP *Remember that many professional actors are extremely nervous before they perform, but because they appear confident and relaxed, people assume that they are.*

Learning to exude confidence

Even if you do feel confident, you will need to *exude* that confidence so that your audience will:

● feel that they are in safe hands
● relax
● be free to concentrate on what you are saying.

81

This becomes a kind of virtuous circle, with the audience's positive response to your confidence further reinforcing that confidence:

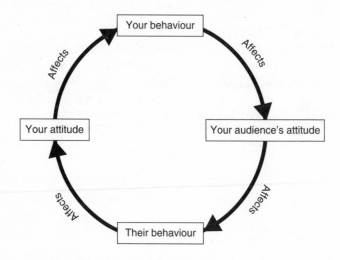

This is sometimes known as the 'Betari Box'.

Memorizing the key points

Memorizing the entire speech is pointless and unnecessary. Besides, if you give speeches frequently, it will be all but impossible to learn them all, and a tiring waste of time. Your speech will come across better if you know it extremely well but work from cue cards to jog your memory, allowing a degree of freshness and spontaneity into your delivery.

There are, however, two potential pitfalls with this approach:

1 You may lose your place on the cue card, or find the cards to be out of sequence.
2 You may read the headline reminder on the cue card and not be able to remember what it refers to.

If you can get into the habit of memorizing your speech's key points, however, even if you do lose your place, or realize that the cue cards have been reordered, you should be able to carry on regardless while buying yourself valuable time to regroup.

If you cannot remember what the card is prompting you to say, it can be trickier, but the situation can be avoided by memorizing not only the headline but some key sub-points, too.

Make sure that you memorize all your speech's headline prompts, as well as at least a couple of sub-points for each one.

Summary

We all know the old adage that 'practice makes perfect' and it's certainly true when it comes to public speaking. The more you can practise, and the more realistic you can make the opportunities, the more you will find yourself gaining in confidence and even beginning to enjoy delivering your speeches.

The act of practising what you will have to do on the day has a wonderfully calming effect, aiding you in being able to project a positive image and to exude confidence – which in turn will help the audience to relax, which will help you to relax.

In order to create this positive circle, you will need to ensure that you are as familiar with your speech as you possibly can be, and that you're confident with the way in which you stand, your deportment, and the way you look overall. By using a mirror to highlight any bad habits you can practise ways to counter them.

Remember, when it comes to public speaking there's no such thing as too much practice.

Tomorrow, Friday, we will look at two issues that can derail the speech-maker, nervousness and tension.

SUNDAY

MONDAY

TUESDAY

WEDNESDAY

THURSDAY

FRIDAY

SATURDAY

Fact-check [answers at the back]

1. How much you will need to practise depends on...
   a) How long your speech is ❏
   b) Previous experience, natural aptitude and confidence level ❏
   c) Your level of stamina ❏
   d) How well you can be seen from the back of the room ❏

2. A recording of your voice sounds different from the way it sounds in your head so you will need to...
   a) Cancel excess background noise ❏
   b) Get used to the sound of your recorded voice when you practise your speech ❏
   c) Add loud background music or sound effects to your recorded voice ❏
   d) Get someone else to record these bits for you ❏

3. Repetition through practice will not only improve your delivery but also...
   a) Make you less afraid of the sound of your own voice ❏
   b) Allow you to learn your speech by heart ❏
   c) Enable you to better control your nerves ❏
   d) Improve hand/tongue co-ordination ❏

4. The more you put in, the more you...
   a) Wish you hadn't ❏
   b) Need to carry ❏
   c) Become tired and irritable ❏
   d) Get out ❏

5. As you gain in confidence you will:
   a) Be able to finish your speech in half the time ❏
   b) Start to look, and feel, more relaxed ❏
   c) Completely lose your nerves ❏
   d) Become a full-time after-dinner speaker ❏

6. Using a mirror to practise will enable you to...
   a) See the different ways in which you fidget ❏
   b) Do your hair at the same time ❏
   c) Keep an eye on your figure ❏
   d) See whether anyone is standing behind you, laughing ❏

7. Practising in front of other people is likely to make you feel...
   a) Like giving up ❏
   b) Awkward and self-conscious ❏
   c) Ill ❏
   d) Like a professional ❏

8. No matter how you feel inside, the audience will perceive only...
   a) What you project to them ❏
   b) What they had imagined you to be like ❏
   c) Themselves ❏
   d) One other ❏

9. By exuding confidence your audience will...
a) Like you better as a person ❏
b) Think you are smug and patronizing ❏
c) Feel that they are in safe hands, and relax ❏
d) Need sunglasses ❏

10. Memorizing your entire speech is...
a) Great fun ❏
b) Achievable in 30 minutes ❏
c) Pointless and unnecessary ❏
d) Useful for reciting at parties ❏

FRIDAY

Dealing with nerves

It's OK to be nervous. In fact, it's a definite advantage for any speech-giver. The reason is a simple biological reaction to your anxiety – your brain triggers the 'fight or flight' mechanism and your body floods your system with adrenalin, giving you an all-important edge – provided you can learn to control it.

Remember that even professional actors get nervous before going on stage, but it's this nervousness which enables them to perform to the very best of their ability. So it is with your speech-giving – the nervous energy the situation creates for you allows you to deliver your speech with power, passion and clarity.

A dull, lifeless speaker is usually one who has given their speech so many times they know it backwards and no longer get nervous, or someone who is overcome with nerves. Any speaker who delivers a dynamic and impassioned speech is almost certain to be nervous, but able to use this to their advantage.

So feeling nervous about giving your speech is a good thing – the trick is to not allow the adrenalin to overpower you, nor the situation to overcome you, but to learn to harness the feeling of fear and use it to your advantage.

Understanding nerves
Why it's good to be nervous

Pretty much everyone gets nervous before a public appearance. Whether it's your first time standing in front of an audience ready to give a speech, or whether it's something you do on a regular basis, you can expect to get nervous. Indeed, as odd as it sounds, you should actually hope to get nervous! This is because the mechanism which creates nervousness is triggered by 'fight or flight' impulses, which provide the energy and 'buzz' which will enable you to give a great performance.

> *'I get nervous when I don't get nervous. If I'm nervous I know I'm going to have a good show.'*
>
> Beyoncé Knowles, US singer

So it's not only perfectly natural to get nervous before giving your speech; it's actually necessary in order to be able to deliver it to the best of your ability.

Some of the tell-tale symptoms you might experience include:

- racing heart
- wobbly legs
- 'butterflies' in your stomach
- 'knotted' feeling in your stomach
- sweating
- weak legs
- feeling of loose bowels
- shaking
- shortness of breath
- tight shoulders
- tight neck
- clenched jaw
- headache
- dry mouth
- feeling sick
- feeling faint or light-headed
- feeling of detachment from your limbs.

After reading this list two reactions are common:

- experiencing some (or all!) of the symptoms
- wishing you hadn't read the list!

It's important to remember that you're unlikely to experience all of these symptoms and, as to be forewarned is to be forearmed, it's better to know what to expect so that you will realize what is happening if you do experience them. Some people are more prone to nervousness than others and will experience it more easily, and some people experience the symptoms more acutely than others (which can include vomiting, diarrhoea and fainting). For most people, though, it's just an uncomfortable feeling of being jittery and on edge, coupled with some mild physical symptoms.

Everyone is different...

Everyone is different and will react differently to each situation, and past performance isn't necessarily a good indicator – some people who can jump out of an aeroplane for a parachute jump, or swim with sharks, without so much as batting an eyelid, go to pieces when they have to speak in public. However it affects you, and to whatever degree, it's important to remember that the reactions caused by the stress of the situation are there for a reason and can be used to your advantage if correctly managed.

What happens when I get nervous?

When the 'fight or flight' response is triggered, several things happen at once, and almost immediately. Some of these are in addition to those we have looked at, while others are their cause:

- Adrenalin and glucose flood into your bloodstream.
- Your heart rate and blood pressure increase.
- Your pupils dilate to allow in as much light as possible.
- The veins in your skin constrict to send more blood to major muscle groups (responsible for the 'chill' sometimes associated with fear).
- Your muscles tense.
- Extra oxygen is taken into your lungs.
- Less essential systems (such as the digestion and immune systems) shut down to allow more energy for emergency functions.

How can I use this response to my advantage?

The sudden introduction of large amounts of adrenalin and glucose into your bloodstream can help to provide you with a 'cutting edge' for your delivery:

- They will provide you with huge amounts of energy (short-term).
- They will provide you with an enhanced level of focus and concentration.
- Your awareness and perception are raised to a new level.
- Your body is being supercharged, ready to give a great performance.

TIP *If you find yourself starting to experience the symptoms of nervousness, try to remember that this is a good thing – then take a few deep breaths to keep the symptoms under control.*

Channelling your adrenalin

In order to make your nervousness work for you, you will need to ensure that you can channel the vast amounts of energy with which your body is being flooded. Learning to control your nerves in this way can be the difference between delivering a fantastic speech with dynamism and élan, and becoming rooted to the spot with fear, unable to speak.

● The first thing is to get used to delivering your speech in front of other people. This will get you used to the feeling of being nervous (albeit to a lesser degree than you are likely to feel when in front of a large audience), and will allow you to see some of the ways in which you respond under pressure.
● Learn to recognize the feelings you experience when you are nervous:
  - What are they?
  - When do they come?
  - How do they manifest themselves?
  - How long do they last?
  - Are they a help or a hindrance?
● Practise seeing your body's physical reaction to the anxiety you are feeling in positive ways where appropriate, and to devise coping strategies where it is not. The table below will help you:

Physical reaction	Positive or negative	How to use it to your advantage	How to cope with it
Heart racing	Positive	Your heart is pumping blood to your muscles ready to give a great, energized speech	
Butterflies in stomach	Positive	Your body is flooding your system with adrenalin ready to tackle the task ahead with energy and élan	
Dry mouth/ scratchy throat	Negative		Have a glass of water to hand
Feeling sick	Positive	Your body is shutting down non-essential processes so that all your energy can be devoted to giving a memorable speech	

Understanding tension

Why it's crucial to release tension

> *'If nerves are a public speaker's best friend, tension is his worst enemy.'*
>
> David Windham, public speaking expert

While nervousness is a positive aspect of public speaking which can help to energize you and to give you that all-important edge, allowing tension to creep into your body can be damaging. But is it possible, under such stressful circumstances, to relax?

> *'True relaxation, which would do me the world of good, does not exist for me.'*
>
> Gustav Klimt, Austrian painter

Relaxation can be hard to come by under such circumstances, and indeed it should be avoided anyway since it will merely counter all the positive aspects of your nervousness. What is possible, however, and certainly desirable, is the ability to rid your body of potentially harmful tension. Tension in your body and in your voice, while attempting to speak in public, will manifest itself in a number of different ways:

Tension in your **body** may:

● make you look nervous
● make you want to fidget

94

- impair your breathing
- make you feel unwell
- make you too rigid
- make your audience nervous.

Tension in your **voice** may:

- make you sound nervous
- make it difficult to control
- make it sound strained
- make you feel unwell
- make it too quiet or too harsh/shrill
- make your audience nervous.

So it's important to try to relax to rid your body – and your voice – of tension. Being relaxed puts you in control of the mechanics of speech-giving, enabling them to work for you and enabling you to give a fantastic, controlled speech.

 TIP *Being nervous is good, but looking nervous isn't – use the relaxation techniques to help overcome this.*

Simple relaxation techniques

The following exercises can be done individually to focus on one specific area, or as a group.

Symptom	Exercise	Result
Tightness in shoulders	Shrug tightly, then relax. Repeat. Move shoulders in large circles.	Promotes relaxation through whole body; aids the appearance of being relaxed; helps to relieve tension from chest, allowing lungs to fill properly.
Tight voice	Yawn – as widely as possible and vocalize with an 'ahhh' sound.	Throat is relaxed; voice does not sound strained; vocal flexibility is improved.

Heart palpitations; shortness of breath	Breathe deeply – hold for ten seconds – and relax. Repeat.	Slows down heart rate; helps to get breathing under control; allows you to sound relaxed and in command.
Tightness in neck	Tip your head forward so that your chin is on your chest – circle head slowly in a large arc. Repeat in opposite direction.	Relieves tension in neck; relaxes throat; improves vocal quality.
Butterflies in stomach; general nervousness	Clench and relax different muscle groups in turn – important ones include forearms, buttocks, quadriceps, stomach, shoulders.	Tempers nervousness; rids tension to promote general relaxation and feeling of well-being; keeps you in control.
Clenched jaw	Swing jaw from side to side, first with mouth open, then closed.	Relaxes jaw; allows the mouth to fully open so sound can freely exit.

The importance of a good warm-up

The importance of a thorough warm-up cannot be underestimated. Not only will it relieve tension but it will prepare you, physically and mentally, for the task ahead. It will also help to channel your adrenalin so that it doesn't overwhelm you, but instead allows you to use it to your advantage. It's imperative that you devote sufficient time to doing a good warm-up so that your body and your voice are ready for the task ahead, and so that you rid both of any damaging tension.

Warming up your **voice** will:

- make it clearer
- allow you to be heard by everyone
- make you sound relaxed
- prevent strain
- put you in control.

Warming up your **body** will:

- help you to relax
- release pent-up adrenalin
- help to prevent you shaking
- get rid of any 'wobbly' feeling
- put you in control.

Remember: professional actors always warm-up before a performance – so should you.

The table below gives some useful warm-up exercises. Over time you will learn which ones are most important for you, and you will be able to tailor them to your needs. Always work within your own limitations and never strain yourself – these should be used as a *gentle* warm-up, not as an exercise routine!

Area of focus	Warm-up exercise
Whole body – general	Stretch up with your whole body, lifting your hands as high as you can, pointing your fingers towards the ceiling – be sure to go up on to the tips of your toes. Feel your whole body stretch – then drop gently down, bending at the waist and keeping your knees slightly bent, so that your head is hanging down in front of your knees and your arms are hanging down in front of your legs. Very slowly unfurl your spine, one vertebra at a time, until you are standing upright, ensuring that your head is the last thing to come up. NB: *Be sure to do this slowly so that you avoid getting dizzy or experiencing 'head rush'.*
Lateral stretch	Stand with your feet shoulder-width apart and let your arms hang down by your sides. Slowly lean to one side allowing your arm to hang freely so that it slides down your leg, then very slowly come upright again. Pause to regain your balance, then repeat on the other side.

Shoulders	Stand with your feet shoulder-width apart and relax your shoulders. Now shrug tightly, lifting your shoulders up to your ears. Hold this for a few seconds, then relax. Repeat. Let your shoulders relax, then try to push them down another few inches, hold for a few seconds, then relax. Repeat. From a neutral position, push your shoulders forward as far as they will comfortably go, hold for a few seconds, then relax. Repeat. From a neutral position, push your shoulders back as far as they will comfortably go, hold for a few seconds, then relax. Repeat. Roll your shoulders in large circles, front to back, then back to front. Repeat.
Neck	Tip your head forward so that your chin is on your chest – circle your head slowly in a large arc until it's back resting comfortably facing forward. Repeat in the opposite direction. NB: *Be sure not to push your head further than is comfortable in any direction, and be particularly careful not to strain your neck muscles by pushing your head back too far.*
Mouth and face	Screw your face up as tightly as possible, trying to make it as small as you can. Relax. Now try to make your face as big as possible, raising your eyebrows and opening your mouth as widely as you can. Relax, and repeat. NB: *This is one to do when you are on your own, as it is impossible not to look comical while doing it!*
Lips	Open your mouth as wide as you can, giving it a firm but comfortable stretch, then pinch your mouth, pushing your lips forward. Repeat. Keeping your teeth together, blow air through your mouth so that your lips ripple (as if you are doing an impression of a horse blowing out!).
Tongue	Stick your tongue out as far as it will go. Move it up, as if you are trying to touch your nose with it. Then move it down, as if you are trying to touch your chin with it. Next move it to the left, as if you are trying to touch your left cheek with it. Finally move it to the right, as if you are trying to touch your right cheek with it. Stick your tongue out as far as it will go and move it in large circles, first one way and then the other.

Jaw	Relax your jaw and swing it gently from side to side, first with your mouth open, then with your mouth closed.
Voice	Stand with your feet shoulder-width apart and relax. Inhale through your nose, slowly and deeply – hold for ten seconds – then exhale slowly, through your mouth. Relax and repeat. Yawn, as widely as possible, and vocalize as you exhale with a long, steady 'ahhh' sound. Take a deep breath and hum, gradually making the sound louder, then open your mouth and turn the sound into a long, steady 'ahhh' sound. Keep this going for as long as you feel comfortable, concentrating on keeping your mouth open and your jaw relaxed so that the sound you create is pure and uninterrupted.

Confidence tricks

There are a number of 'tricks of the trade' employed by professional public speakers to give them an air of confidence. Remember that if you appear confident your audience will feel that they are in safe hands and will relax – allowing you to do the same. These are some of the most popular techniques used by professional speakers:

● Know your speech thoroughly – and stick to it.
● Have a glass of water to hand.
● Don't drink alcohol to calm your nerves – it can make you more relaxed but it also dulls your senses. Use the relaxation techniques instead.
● Fight the temptation to rush your speech:
  – speak slowly
  – don't forget to pause.
● If wearing a tie, undo your top button (hidden behind the tie).
● Pick out one person at a time from your audience and deliver that part of the speech directly to them.
● If you feel nervous, picture the audience members naked!
● Keep your feet still.
● Keep your hands firmly planted to, or resting on, the lectern, or firmly gripping your cue cards.
● Don't speak over laughter.

The confidence ladder

As you gain in experience of speaking in public, you will find that you also gain in confidence about doing so:

Gain in confidence → Voice becomes stronger → Voice becomes clearer → Diction improves → Get a positive reputation → Gain charisma → Desire to do more public speaking → Gain in confidence...

Two-minute warm-ups that can be done anywhere

There is no substitute for a good, thorough warm-up. It will help to rid your body and your voice of potentially damaging tension while preparing them for the task ahead, and employing a familiar routine will help to calm your nerves. So why would you ever want to do a warm-up lasting only two minutes?

● **You may not be able to do your warm-up immediately prior to giving your speech.** Is it best to do it as close as possible to the moment of delivery, but if there has been a delay then a quick two-minute warm-up is perfect for getting things back up to speed, and provided the delay hasn't been too long this sort of 'turbo-charge' warm-up should suffice.

● **Sometimes, despite your best efforts, it's impossible to complete a proper warm-up** (e.g. if you weren't expecting to speak and someone suddenly asks you to do so at zero notice). In this situation a two-minute warm-up, basic as it is, is certainly better than nothing, and it will provide you with the opportunity to gather your thoughts and focus on your speech while preparing your body and your voice for the undertaking.

SUNDAY
MONDAY
TUESDAY
WEDNESDAY
THURSDAY
FRIDAY
SATURDAY

 These super-quick warm-ups can be performed anywhere – if there is nowhere more suitable to hand, then the venue's toilets will do perfectly well.

Physical warm-up

Deep breathing

- Stand up tall, relax your body and breathe in deeply.
- Hold for ten seconds and slowly release.
- Repeat five times.

Stretching

- Stretch as high as you can reach, on tiptoes. Relax.
- Stretch your arms as wide as you can. Relax.
- Repeat five times.

Scrunching and stretching your face

- Scrunch and stretch your face really tight, pinching it in. Relax.
- Scrunch and stretch your face as wide as possible, lifting your eyebrows and opening your mouth. Relax.
- Repeat five times.

Vocal warm-up

Yawning

- Open your mouth really wide and yawn loudly, vocalizing the sound as you exhale.
- Repeat five times.

Humming

- Hum one steady note, starting softly and growing louder.
- Repeat, but this time open your mouth widely allowing the sound out fully.
- Repeat five times.

Lip and tongue mobility

● Stick your tongue out and move it in large circles.
● Repeat your favourite tongue-twister.

Summary

One of the main stumbling blocks for anyone unused to speaking in public is the act of controlling their nerves when standing up in front of an audience. While it's good to be nervous, it's not good to look nervous or to be overwhelmed by nerves, so learning to control them is crucial; and by doing so you can harness their considerable power and energy and use them to your advantage.

By employing the techniques described in this chapter to harness the energy and edge gifted to you by nervousness you will be able to minimize the likelihood of having the occasion marred by a debilitating 'attack' of nerves, while at the same time elevating your speech-giving to a whole new level. In order to make sure that you give yourself, and your speech, the best possible chance of success you should aim to master the techniques as fully as possible, and as soon as possible, so that when you need them they will be second nature to you, ready and waiting – an essential part of your speech-giving arsenal.

Tomorrow is the last day of your seven-day journey towards being a great speech-giver, and we will be looking at the common pitfalls and how to avoid them.

SUNDAY
MONDAY
TUESDAY
WEDNESDAY
THURSDAY
FRIDAY
SATURDAY

Fact-check [answers at the back]

1. It's good to get nervous before delivering your speech because...
a) Looking nervous will elicit sympathy from the audience ❏
b) Shaking helps to control your voice ❏
c) It charges your body with energy ❏
d) It helps you to lose weight ❏

2. Tell-tale symptoms of nervousness commonly experienced include...
a) Blackouts ❏
b) Stomach feeling 'knotted' or having butterflies in it ❏
c) Double-vision ❏
d) A feeling of tranquillity and calm ❏

3. Learning to channel your adrenalin is important because...
a) You can save it for later ❏
b) It can get messy if not reined in ❏
c) It can be used to your advantage ❏
d) Otherwise you might become hysterical ❏

4. Tension in your body may...
a) Make you feel relaxed ❏
b) Be good for your voice ❏
c) Make you appear taller ❏
d) Make you look, and feel, nervous ❏

5. Tension in your voice may...
a) Make it louder ❏
b) Make your voice sound strained, or shrill ❏
c) Make it clearer ❏
d) Give it a pleasing tone and resonance ❏

6. Being relaxed puts you in control of...
a) The audience ❏
b) The mechanics of speech-giving ❏
c) Your company ❏
d) Your finances ❏

7. Being nervous is good but...
a) It's not that good ❏
b) It's not for everyone ❏
c) Looking nervous isn't ❏
d) Only at weekends ❏

8. A good warm-up will...
a) Relieve tension and prepare you for the task ahead ❏
b) Help to counter the air conditioning ❏
c) Be invaluable preparation for running a marathon ❏
d) Inspire the audience to get fit ❏

9. It's inadvisable to drink alcohol before giving your speech because...
a) It's usually very expensive at large venues ❏
b) You may be so nervous you won't want to stop ❏
c) If the lights fail, you may have to recite your entire speech by heart ❏
d) It dulls your senses, and diminishes your capacity to give a great speech ❏

10. Two-minute warm-ups can be useful because...

a) Warming-up for any longer will tire you ❑

b) After two minutes your body can't get any warmer ❑

c) They can be done quickly, anywhere ❑

d) Warming-up for any longer is just a waste of time ❑

SATURDAY

Common mistakes and how to avoid them

Despite all your best efforts, dedicated practice, and careful preparation for giving your speech, it's a fact of life that something can still go wrong with some part of your speech-giving at some point. This is almost inevitable if you give speeches regularly due to the number of possible chances for it to happen; and even if you give speeches only rarely the odds are still high, since you won't have had the necessary practice to build up a store of experience which can help to prevent the possible pitfalls and pratfalls of speech-giving.

So either way, it's highly likely that you will be faced with challenging moments and experiences with which you will have to deal. Part of the key to doing this successfully lies in being as prepared as possible, thinking through all the eventualities which might occur to trip you up. Even though you won't be able to picture them all, thinking through as many as possible will help to get you into the habit of being ready to deal with the unexpected.

The other part is adopting the best mindset to spot mistakes early and deal with them swiftly, so that they will have the minimum possible impact on your speech, or even go unnoticed.

Trying to ad lib

Ad libbing – making unscripted remarks off the cuff – is a skill best left to the professionals. They make it look easy but don't be fooled – it's an incredibly difficult art to master and, unless you can do it brilliantly, it can all too easily go wrong and make you look amateurish.

You are almost always better off sticking to the script. Besides, if you have worked hard to write a great speech, and practised hard to be able to deliver it with dynamism and professionalism, why wouldn't you want to stick to the plan and give a speech which you know is great?

TIP *It's extremely difficult to ad lib really well, and if it's not brilliant it can all too easily fall flat.*

The biggest danger with ad libbing is that in the heat of the moment, under the pressure to perform and filled with adrenalin, you may say something you wish you hadn't. Many speeches have been ruined in this way – and even careers.

Some of the most common reasons for ad libbing are that you:

- feel the speech is going badly and needs a 'lift'
- feel under pressure to be funny or to keep the audience entertained
- feel insecure about your material
- are answering a question from the floor.

This last point is worthy of further consideration. Obviously, you can't prepare your answers to questions you haven't heard, so how can you ensure that you don't say something you might later regret?

The answer lies in the preparation of your material. If you know your subject inside out, then there is no reason why you shouldn't be able to answer any question you may be asked without straying into dangerous territory; and if you don't know the answer it's better to say so than to guess (and risk being shown to be wrong, perhaps in front of the entire audience).

Crucially, you should always keep your answers short and to the point – it's when you begin to ramble and waffle that errors are likely to creep in, and that includes saying something which is factually correct but which you really don't want your audience to hear.

TIP *It only takes an unguarded second to say the wrong thing – but you might regret it for ever.*

Allowing interruptions

Heckling during business speeches is uncommon but not unheard of, and usually occurs during a question and answer session. Someone may call out their question unbidden, or ask a further question once you have moved on to someone else's question, and all too easily you can succumb to the 'snowball effect'. This is where you allow one person to interrupt your speech, in whichever way, and then others quickly jump on the bandwagon – and before you know it you have been made redundant, left to just stand at the front looking awkward and trying to regain control of the situation.

It's crucial, therefore, that you retain control of the situation at all times, for your sake and for the sake of the audience. If you allow a situation of heckling or multiple calling out to occur, several unwanted things happen:

- The focus and direction of your speech are lost.
- The flow and momentum of your speech are lost.
- Your audience is left isolated and bewildered.
- You have lost control and will almost certainly become more nervous.
- You will end up firefighting, with all the structure of your argument eroded.

The most alarming aspect of this situation is the speed with which it can happen; and if you don't nip it in the bud right away it can very quickly spiral out of control. The key, then, is to ensure that you are always:

- alert to the possibility of it happening
- ready to deal with it quickly and firmly
- determined not to let it happen, even if that means risking appearing rude by talking over your audience to restore order.

Regaining control

Don't be afraid to take command of the situation and speak over people to regain control – your audience will be grateful that you did, and you will appear confident and in command. This will, in turn, help to settle your nerves, and you will have turned a potentially damaging situation into one which has allowed you to shine.

Straying from the subject

'His speeches left the impression of an army of pompous phrases moving over the landscape in search of an idea.'

Anon.

If yiu ahve carefully written your speech and diligently worked on perfecting your delivery, you are far better off sticking to the 'script' – wandering off at a tangent is a great way to add an unnecessary element of uncertainty to an occasion which was otherwise meticulously planned and practised. Depending on how far from your core themes you stray, you might find you are covering tangential topics on which you had not intended to encroach, or you may even wander away from your subject altogether! Veering away from your intended speech will:

At best:

- dilute the contents of your speech
- lose the focus of your message
- make you seem less competent
- confuse the audience.

At worst:

- have little or nothing to do with your subject
- appear self-indulgent
- make your speech unreasonably long
- leave the audience bewildered or bored.

Maintaining good speech-giving discipline will ensure that your speech always remains focused and targeted, and that you appear confident and in control – so stick to the subject and keep to the script.

Give the best speech you're able to give by delivering the speech you had intended to deliver.

Relying on, or misusing, technology

You may well wish to employ some form of technology in your speech, and indeed this can be an excellent way of communicating information quickly and easily, or more directly and accurately than would otherwise be possible. This can also be a good way to add variety, create intrigue and, importantly, to give you a break! However – and it's a big 'however' – all technology is susceptible to Murphy's Law: 'If it can go wrong it will go wrong!' So always make sure you have a back-up to hand in an appropriate format, to prevent your speech grinding to an unscheduled stop, e.g. if you intend to show a PowerPoint presentation, ensure that you have a print-out of it to hand – but also have all the data available in a format which allows you to give out the salient points, without floundering and trying to describe each slide.

It's also important to remember that while the inclusion of technological aids can help to elevate your speech, it should never be its mainstay. It's best used sparingly, and only when it's unquestionably the best way to communicate the information you wish to deliver to your audience, or when you wish to inject some variety into your speech. It can help to give you a pause during your speech (particularly useful if your speech is lengthy), but it must never be apparent that this is why you have included it! Any technology you employ:

Must be:

✔ relevant
✔ audible/visible to everyone
✔ the best way to communicate specific information
✔ ready to start and finish instantly
✔ clearly relevant.

Must not be:

✕ the mainstay of your speech
✕ generic
✕ gimmicky
✕ used as 'filler'
✕ relied upon!

Another common pitfall with using technology to bolster a speech is over-use. This can:

● make your speech cluttered
● slow you down
● draw emphasis away from what you're saying.

It should therefore be kept to a minimum and used sparingly, only being included if it's:

● completely relevant
● entirely appropriate
● going to complement your speech – not undermine it.

TIP *Contact the venue in advance to let them know of your technological requirements, and to determine whether or not they can be accommodated, and if you will need to bring everything or if it's all supplied. Be careful to ensure there is an adequate power supply, not only in terms of wattage but also location, and that there are a sufficient number of power sockets where you need them.*

What to do if you begin to feel overwhelmed

'The best way to gain self-confidence is to do what you are afraid to do.'

Anon.

Despite diligent practice and preparation, you won't be able to replicate exactly what it will be like on the day due to a number of factors which are either beyond your control or else all but impossible to create in advance, such as assembling a suitably large audience to hear your speech. And by not having experienced the conditions exactly, prior to giving your speech, there is always the possibility that the occasion might overwhelm you.

By thinking through the reasons for this in advance, and by being as prepared as possible to combat them, you can minimize their impact and give yourself the best possible chance of staying on top of the situation.

In addition to an unexpectedly large audience, other factors to be aware of include:

- **N**ervousness – you may have experienced a degree of this when practising but you are almost bound to experience it to a greater degree when you are giving your speech 'for real'.
- **A**tmosphere – each venue, and each audience, creates its own unique atmosphere. These can help to lift your performance but can also threaten to undermine it if it all becomes too much.
- **S**ense of occasion – the speech you are giving may be important for your company, for the occasion you are presenting at, and for you. The more important the occasion, the more likely it is that you may feel overwhelmed by it.

- **A**udience – will there be someone in the audience you are particularly nervous about presenting to? Might there be a surprise VIP guest on the day?

Remembering **'NASA'** will help you to be ready for extra pressures you may experience on the day – fortunately, combatting them is not rocket science!

Similarly, remembering **'SPACE'** may help you to maintain a cool, calm temperament, and to keep your composure, whatever the situation:

- **S**tand tall, with your feet firmly planted, shoulder-width apart, and maintain a good posture.
- **P**lace a glass of water to hand to keep your mouth from drying.
- **A**void drinking alcohol to calm your nerves – it doesn't work and leaves you less in control.
- **C**ontrol your breathing – take several deep breaths before you begin, and one whenever you pause.
- **E**nsure that you take your time – don't rush, and pause when you need to, to compose yourself.

Becoming distracted

You may have practised until you are almost perfect with your speech-giving every time you run through it, but rest assured that on the day, given the additional external factors that will impact your delivery, it's very easy to become distracted. If you are used to attending speeches then you will probably have seen it for yourself – a speaker who allows their attention to wander, even for just a second, and gets caught out by not realizing that a film presentation was about to end, or by not being able to find their place in their notes, or even by not being able to remember what they were talking about! It happens, but it needn't happen to you.

One of the most common reasons for a sudden loss of concentration is the occurrence of negative thoughts. One minute your speech is going really well and you are getting your nerves under control, the next doubts are starting to creep in and you are beginning to wonder whether the audience is enjoying what you are saying. Are they finding it interesting? Useful? Are they wishing they hadn't come?

And the next thing you know there is an awkward silence as everyone waits for you to continue with the speech. In order to prevent this, it is crucial that you approach your speech with the most positive attitude possible. You have worked hard on writing a great speech; you have worked hard on delivering a great speech; now all you have to do is to believe in yourself and maintain your concentration and your focus.

Another typical reason for losing your concentration is the other side of the same coin – complacency. Your speech is going really well, you have every reason to believe that the audience is thoroughly engaged with what you are saying, and you are so relieved that you allow your guard to drop. It takes only a second and suddenly you are floundering, and kicking yourself for allowing these self-congratulatory thoughts into your head.

The trick to not letting your mind wander like this is to keep focused on what you are saying, and to have decided before you begin that you are not going to try to read the audience's reaction to your speech while you are still giving it, but to leave that until after it is finished.

The third pitfall people fall into when distracted is allowing themselves to ramble. You shouldn't be reading your speech verbatim, but taking the headline notes on your cue cards and expanding on them. This means that you have the licence to either keep your message short and to the point, or else to ramble – and risk losing your audience's interest in the process.

So make sure that you have an idea of how much time it should take to cover each of your points and try to ensure that you don't allow yourself to go beyond it.

Summary

Although it's impossible to ensure that you will never, ever, make a mistake – indeed, it's highly probable that at some point you *will* make a mistake – it's possible to ensure that these are kept to a minimum, and that you know how to deal with them when they do occur so that their negative impact on your speech is minimized. You can also minimize the likelihood of needing to add unrehearsed elements to your material by ensuring that you don't rush your speech; and by taking just one question at a time, and by dictating the quantity of the input from the audience, you can maintain control of the situation.

Make sure that any technology on which you rely is working properly and can be catered for at the venue (and never, ever rely on anything which relies on batteries!) and keep to your subject and to the way in which you have rehearsed your speech to ensure that the material won't let you down.

Keep your focus, take some deep breaths if you begin to feel overwhelmed, and concentrate on delivering your speech the way you have practised, and you will have every reason to believe that your speech will go really well – mistakes or no mistakes.

SUNDAY
MONDAY
TUESDAY
WEDNESDAY
THURSDAY
FRIDAY
SATURDAY

Fact-check [answers at the back]

1. Ad libbing is a skill...
a) Which can be mastered in minutes ❑
b) Best left to the professionals ❑
c) You should aim to employ in every speech ❑
d) Essential to public speaking ❑

2. The biggest danger with ad libbing is that...
a) In the heat of the moment you may say something you wish you hadn't ❑
b) It can become addictive ❑
c) You may be tempted to recite stories not connected to your speech ❑
d) The audience might want to join in ❑

3. Allowing interruptions to your speech can ruin...
a) Your day ❑
b) You chances of promotion ❑
c) The flow and momentum of your speech ❑
d) Your ability to get it over with quickly ❑

4. Wandering off at a tangent to your speech is a great way to...
a) Underline the key points ❑
b) Explore new territory ❑
c) Keep the interest of anyone who has heard it before ❑
d) Add an unnecessary element of uncertainty to your delivery ❑

5. Veering away from your intended speech will...
a) Add a welcome element of intrigue and mystery ❑
b) Lose its focus and confuse the audience ❑
c) Allow you to cover multiple topics ❑
d) Allow you to save some material for another time ❑

6. It can be useful to incorporate technology into your speech in order to...
a) Use up time so you don't have to prepare such a long speech ❑
b) Communicate specific information concisely and clearly ❑
c) Show off your mastery of information technology ❑
d) Keep your audience awake ❑

7. Technology should only be employed in your speech when...
a) You run out of ideas ❑
b) You become bored of your own material ❑
c) It's completely relevant and entirely appropriate ❑
d) It's free ❑

8. You should never, ever rely on...
a) Anything which relies on batteries ❑
b) The venue to provide lunch ❑
c) Your own ability to give a great speech ❑
d) Your boss ❑

9. If you begin to feel overwhelmed by the occasion you should...
a) Reconsider undertaking public speaking engagements ❏
b) Stop, and seek medical help ❏
c) Control your breathing, and take your time ❏
d) Faint ❏

10. A little humour in your speech is great, but too much may...
a) Create so much laughter your speech can't be heard ❏
b) Be inappropriate and come back to haunt you ❏
c) Underline your key themes ❏
d) Be a blessing in disguise ❏

7 × 7

Seven top tips

1 There are three parts to every speech: tell your audience what you are going to tell them; tell them; and then tell them what you have told them.

2 Get into the habit of always noting down your ideas as and when they occur to you, no matter where you are or what you are doing. You may not remember them later.

3 Divide your speech into manageable sections, and pare each one down to the bare bones. Then keep it simmering until only the richest material remains.

4 Your speech should be the right length – not for you, but for your audience.

5 Breathe deeply. This will help to slow you down, and calm your nerves, as well as supporting your voice for effective delivery.

6 Rehearse in front of other people, and begin at the earliest opportunity.

7 Memorize the key points of your speech – but don't learn it by heart.

Seven ways to control nerves

1 Remember that being nervous is a good thing – the energy it creates allows you to deliver your speech with power, passion and dynamism. Don't be afraid of nerves.

2 Learn to recognize the feelings you experience when you are nervous, and practise seeing your body's physical reaction to the anxiety you are feeling in a positive light.

3 Use simple relaxation techniques immediately before giving your speech to rid your body of tension, and to ensure that you don't look nervous.

4 Thoroughly warm up your body, and especially your voice, before giving your speech.

5 Check out the venue as soon as possible, and make sure that you have somewhere to rest your notes, and a place for a glass of water.
6 Try out the 'confidence tricks' to learn which ones work best for you – then memorize them, and practise them often.
7 Remember to keep things in proportion – everyone gets nervous when speaking in public, but nobody ever died of it!

Seven pitfalls to avoid

1 When it comes to speeches, longer doesn't mean better. Keep it short, sharp and focused.
2 Silly gimmicks, unnecessary props and questionable humour have no place in a good speech.
3 Ad libbing. Even the very best comedians sometimes come unstuck doing this; the rest of us shouldn't even try.
4 Don't gabble.
5 Frequent coughing, nervous laughter and fidgeting are sure signs of a nervous speaker. Keep your body and your voice under control.
6 Never permit interruptions or succumb to distractions.
7 Do not stray from the script – this will often lead to a speaker straying from the subject.

Seven things to do today

1 Great speeches aren't written – they're rewritten. Allow yourself plenty of time by getting your speechwriting under way at the earliest opportunity, and then improve it continually with subsequent amendments.
2 Ask colleagues, bosses, stakeholders and so on whether they want to be consulted on your speech, and whether there is anything specific that they want you to include.
3 Find out who your audience will be – if you know whom you will be giving your speech to, you can pitch it appropriately.
4 Begin practising speaking out loud – and loudly – whenever you are on your own. The more often you do it, the more normal it will become to you.

5 Find some colleagues to whom you can practise giving your speech, and from whom you can receive constructive criticism.
6 Start practising giving your speech in front of a full-length mirror.
7 Buy some cue cards, and start practising reading from them while maintaining eye contact with your audience.

Seven ways to look like a pro

1 Start and finish strongly.
2 Make eye contact with your audience, often, and throughout your speech.
3 Stick to the script.
4 Colour your voice through inflection, and vary your pace, tone, pitch and volume.
5 Never be afraid to pause. It can help to undermine a point, or to build expectation and focus on what you are about to say.
6 Don't rush your delivery.
7 Command the space. Look confident by walking purposefully to the podium, looking your audience in the eye, and remembering to smile.

Seven inspiring speakers

1 Nelson Mandela (1918–2013), South African President 1994–9, anti-apartheid activist and revolutionary
2 Steve Jobs (1955–2011), entrepreneur, and cofounder, Chairman and CEO of Apple Inc.
3 Winston Churchill (1874–1965), British Prime Minister 1940–45 and 1951–5
4 Mother Theresa (1910–97), founder of the Missionaries of Charity Roman Catholic religious order
5 Martin Luther King, Jr. (1929–68), civil rights campaigner, activist and humanitarian
6 John F. Kennedy (1917–63), President of the United States of America 1961–3

7 Billy Crystal (1948–present), actor, comedian and nine-times Master of Ceremonies at the Academy Awards (Oscars)

Seven great quotes

1 'A speech is like a woman's skirt: it needs to be long enough to cover the subject matter, but short enough to hold the audience's attention.' Anon.

2 'How often in life we complete a task that was beyond the capability of the person we were when we started it.' Robert Brault

3 'It takes one hour of preparation for each minute of presentation time.' Wayne Burgraff

4 'His speeches left the impression of an army of pompous phrases moving over the landscape in search of an idea.' Anon.

5 'Be sincere, be brief, be seated.' Franklin Delano Roosevelt

6 'There are certain things in which mediocrity is not to be endured, such as poetry, music, painting, public speaking.' Jean de La Bruyère

7 'Always be shorter than anybody dared to hope.' Lord Reading

Answers

Sunday: 1b; 2d; 3d; 4b; 5a; 6b; 7c; 8c; 9d; 10a

Monday: 1c; 2a; 3a; 4b; 5c; 6a; 7b; 8c; 9d; 10b

Tuesday: 1d; 2a; 3c; 4b; 5c; 6d; 7b; 8c; 9d; 10b

Wednesday: 1a; 2b; 3c; 4a; 5b; 6d; 7b; 8a; 9c; 10a

Thursday: 1b; 2b; 3c; 4d; 5b; 6a; 7b; 8a; 9c; 10c

Friday: 1c; 2b; 3c; 4d; 5b; 6b; 7c; 8a; 9d; 10c

Saturday: 1b; 2a; 3c; 4d; 5b; 6b; 7c; 8a; 9c; 10b